UNBROKEN SPIRIT

The life of

WILLIAM BOXHAL

Convict 3744

by

Brian Peachey

HESPERIAN
PRESS

2000
HESPERIAN PRESS
P.O. BOX 317
VICTORIA PARK 6979
65 OATS STREET
CARLISLE 6101
WESTERN AUSTRALIA.

ISBN 0 85905 275 3

Hesperian books are available direct from the publisher. For a full catalogue of Hesperian books on Australiana, natural history, military history, exploration, Aboriginal ethnography, bush verse and gold prospecting, please forward a self-addressed, stamped business size envelope (220 x 110) to the above address.

All Hesperian books are printed on quality paper and will not discolour with age. They are section sewn in signatures, the pages will not drop out and the binding will not crack. This book is made to last.

Dedicated

to
Vivienne,
my mother-in-law, the
great-grand-daughter of William Boxhal.

Acknowledgments

Among the many people I have to thank for assistance to complete this work, the person to whom I owe most is my wife, Miriam, who for a year showed great patience and tolerance to a preoccupied husband, who should otherwise have been earning money. She also read the early manuscript with valuable input and painstakingly did the index. John Kehoe, a "Rat of Tobruk" and the oldest living descendant of the Boxhals, read the manuscript and like the good school principal that he was, corrected some twenty errors.

My son, Dr Brendan Peachey, who while at the University of Liverpool did valuable research at Preston, the Lancashire Record Office and the Public Record Office, the National Archives at Kew.

I am grateful for the courteous and helpful assistance given by -the staff at Battye Library of WA History, the Alexander Library , the Public Records Office of Western Australia and the University of Western Australia Library; especially to my daughter, Lucy who is employed at the latter. The Right Reverend Placid Spearrit, O.S.B.,the Abbot of New Norcia, gave me permission to research the records of the Abbey and use several photographs. The New Norcia archivist, Wendy McKinley was most generous with her time and gave me invaluable assistance.

To my friend, the great Australian writer and poet, Hal Colebatch, I owe a debt for his valuable advice and guidance.

The present owner of the property that Boxhal once owned, Ronald Nixon, kindly gave permission to enter his property and directed me to the foundations of the homes that Boxhal built.

To Murray McDonald, artist and friend for half a century, I am grateful for his excellent illustrations and the design of the cover.

The descendants are indebted to various persons who collected the genealogical details.

Contents

List of Illustrations

Introduction

My interest in the life of William Boxhal was generated by the family of my wife, who as late as 1979, seemed to know little of the history of the man they called grandpa Boxhal. Research at Battye Library revealed he was the son of a convict, who arrived in Western Australia in 1856. The stigma of one's father being a convict caused many of the second generation not to pass on the knowledge to the subsequent generations.

In searching into the history of the convict, William Boxhal, I developed a deep sympathy for him because of the life he suffered in appalling conditions in early nineteenth century England, his degrading incarceration and his transportation to Australia on a small, crowded, convict ship. But I came to admire the strength of the man. This man, when released to work in a strange harsh land, had no material possessions and was a convicted criminal in a colony established by English gentlemen. By sheer determination and hard work he purchased land for cash, became a successful farmer, raised a large family and left a great progeny.

When one writes a history of a pioneer who lived a century and a half earlier, it is usual to refer to diaries, letters, trading records, receipts and the like; but in the case of William Boxhal, there is little such evidence.

The primary source material is the convict records and official documents, such as certificates of titles to land, contracts of employment, the record of his marriage; the births, deaths and marriages of his family and his last will and testament.

Alexander Library and the J. S. Battye Library deserve praise for having preserved such a wealth of historic documents, but, as is stated in the index to the Register of Convicts : "Most volumes have been damaged to some extent, damp, silverfish, missing pages etc".

Based on very substantial evidence, I have formed my opinions on the way he lived and the work he did to achieve the material success as so few former convicts did.

The degrading privation of imprisonment and tranportation, which destroyed many, was a strange twist of fate; Boxhal was a fortunate man, because he could take advantage of opportunities in a new undeveloped land that would have not come his way in England.

The Swan River Colony, established in 1829 on the western coast of Australia, was constituted a penal settlement in 1850, one year after the last British convict had been transported to New South Wales. The transporting of convicts to Western Australia began with the arrival of the *Scindian* on 1 June 1850, and continued until the *Hougoumont* discharged its cargo of 279 on 10 January 1868. In all 9718 convicts were sent to Western Australia. Only about 300 were able to overcome the debasing conditions and succeed; William Boxhal was one of this number.

Little is known of the early life of Boxhal in England. He was baptised in the village of Godalming in Surrey in 1832. He suffered poverty and received little if any formal education, but worked from an early age as a blacksmith. He was arrested for stealing in Fulwood in Lancashire in 1852, tried in Preston and sentenced to ten years transportation.

The spelling of his name varies in the records. He was baptised William Boxall, but in his will he uses the name William Charles Boxhal. The baptismal records use the spelling Boxall, this was also used when he was tried and also used in the convict records; when his first son, William, was baptised the spelling recorded was Boxhall (a spelling the son used throughout his life); when he was married, when he purchased and sold land and in his will and death certificate it was Boxhal, which is the spelling I will use.

There are other conflicting records, possibly caused by either illiteracy or verbal inaccuracies. Unfortunately there are no copies of letters to his family. If there were any they have not been discovered. There does seem to be a silence among the second generation about their convict roots. This silence and the illiteracy of the first (and also the second) generation, resulted in few written records.

It is a unique story of the human spirit being unbroken and rising above adversity.

1

Early Life

Because of the complex changes caused by what has customarily been called the "Industrial Revolution", the rapid increase in population and other factors, periods of the nineteenth century were bad and degrading for the labouring class in England. Those who lacked valued skills, education and property, were some of the most miserable and poverty stricken in its history. Many suffered the two deadly prongs of unemployment and the escalating cost of food.

The agrarian changes brought about by the various Enclosure Acts were a turning-point in British history. The land was made to yield more food, but the class of peasant small land holders became landless labourers and drifted to the towns.

The industrial revolution gave Britain a supremacy over other nations. Without such industrial advantage, Britain could not have defeated Napoleon, or built up its colonial empire. It also increased the wealth of the merchant class and the aristocracy, but in the first half of the 19th century it caused thousands to be thrown into unemployment and unrelieved destitution. In the new industrial towns, men and women were toiling up to seventeen hours a day and were reduced to the tragedy of exposing their children, some as young as five, to the brutality of work in the cotton mills and mines.

The working-class was largley unable to improve its lot. Not only were they disenfranchised, but Pitt's Combination Act forbade any combination of workmen to act together for higher wages or any of the other normal objects of Trade Unions. The majority of the Members in the Parliament were fearful of an uprising similiar to the French Revolution.

What became known as the Condition-of-England question was according to Sir Arthur Bryant:

> the spectacle of women with blackened faces with tears courseing down their faces as they dragged their loads up pit ladders, of work-

dizzy cotton spinners mangled in the shafts of unfenced machinery, of workhouse children rented by frugal minded overseers to rough north-country mill owners who treated them like beasts of burden. They treated them worse, for while only a fool would maltreat his horse, a manufacturer could always replace crippled or the prematurely senile by further supplies of cheap labour that cost him nothing but their keep. A Lancashire cotton manufacturer's responsibility to his employees began and ended at the factory gate.(1)

The eminent English writer Sir Walter Scott described the situation:

A man may assemble five hundred workmen one week and dismiss them the next, without having any connection with them than to receive a week's work for a week's wages, nor any solicitude about their future fate than if they were so many old shuttles. (2)

The long-running, costly Napoleonic war had made the situation worse and sapped the wealth at the disposal of the Government, which in any case seemed to be incompetent, bigoted or oblivious to the plight of the poor. The war also drove up the cost of basic food, especially bread, caused by the escalation in the price of imported wheat. This compelled some districts to adopt what was known as the "Speenhamland system" a demoralising form of poor relief, which was supposed to supplement a labourer's wages in accordance with the number of his children and the price of bread. What was even more degrading was the establishment of poor workhouses, where the young and the aged, respectable and depraved, sane and insane were all too often herded together into the same dingy establishment.

The deplorable state of social injustice suffered by a quarter of the population and the disregard for fundamental human rights was an indictment of the Governments led by Pitt the younger and other Tory, Whig and Liberal leaders.

There were commendable efforts of a small number of Members of Parliament and other reformers, but it was not until 1870 that the Education Act was passed that laid the foundations for a national system of elementary education. And in 1871 the Combination Act was repealed and the Parliament passed the Trade Union Act, which gave Trade Unions limited legal rights.

Some historians have tried to excuse the leaders of this time, but none can ignore the deplorable conditions that ordinary people suffered during the early part of the nineteenth century.

William Boxhal was born into this time.

The small village of Godalming, with its narrow streets and wood

The Church of Saints Peter and Paul, Godalming where William
Boxhal was baptised. (Photograph courtesy Barbara Mitting)

High Street Godalming, which has changed little since the nineteenth century.
(Photograph courtesy Barbara Mitting)

3

decorated brick houses built in the 17th century, is located on the River Wey in Surrey, two miles south of Guildford and about 20 miles from London. It was once the centre of the Surrey wool industry. The most dominant feature is the large, centuries old stone church of Saints Peter and Paul, where a blacksmith, Thomas Boxhal and Matilda Fegent were married on 11 April, 1831. In the same church their first born son, William was baptised on 12 February, 1832.

The Boxhal family expanded rapidly; Eunice was born on 5 January, 1834; Johanna on 28 June, 1835 and Mary Ann on 11 December, 1837. All were born in Godalming. The infant Mary Ann died three weeks after her birth. Their fifth child Matilda was born on 10 March,1839 in Camberwell, London. The next two were born in Croydon, Surrey; Henry on 8 August, 1841 and Thomas on 5 November, 1843. Their last child Alfred was born in Deptford on the Thames on 4 January, 1846. (3) The movement of Thomas Boxhal and his young family seems to indicate an instability caused by the continual search for employment. Thomas Boxhal may have worked as a blacksmith at the Deptford Victualling Yard or the Deptford Naval Dockyard, which was where most of the transport ships were fitted out to accommodate convicts.

Deptford is part of the inner city of the greater London, which the nineteenth century commentators Henry Mayhew and John Binny described as " a city of antithesis ... where life itself is painted in pure black and white and where the the very extremes of society are seen in greater force than anywhere else." They refer to "exceeding wealth" and "exceeding misery" and that London had "the greatest amount of human wretchedness to be seen concentrated within it; wretchedness, too, that is made to look still more wretched simply from the fact of it being associated with the most abundant comfort in the world." (4)

Six months after the birth of Alfred, tragedy struck the Boxhal family; Thomas died at Hursts Buildings in the village of Lewisham at the age of 36. The cause of death was 'fever due to ulcerated bowel'. (5) He died only a short distance from where the ship *William Hammond* sailed from England, on which his eldest son, William, was transported as a convict to Australia.

William Boxhal, who followed his father's trade as a smith was fourteen when his father died. He had most likely been working for some years and the burden of caring for his mother and the family fell to him. It was a huge task for such a young man in the deprived society, where unemployment was the norm.

Like many in southern England, he eventually went north to Lancashire, where there were more opportunities in the industrial towns. The port town of Preston was one of the growing industrial centres. By 1850 there were some forty cotton factories using half-starved sweated labour, some of whom were poor Irish immigrants, escaping across the Irish Sea from the disaster of the potato famine.

Unemployment was chronic and the living conditions of the poor in Lancashire, especially in Preston, were appallingly bad.

Michael Cannon writes of the times that "social conditions were breeding a race of felons ... Many men have been converted into criminals in the aftermath of the Napoleonic wars, with 400,000 hardened soldiers and sailors suddenly thrown on to a shrinking employment market ... The contrast between the lives of the rich and poor is probably greater than at any time during England's history."(6)

There are no statistics that measure the sum total of human misery, but the evidence was that in the mid-nineteenth century Britain, in the industrial towns, such as Preston, large sections of the population were living in abject poverty. The founders of Communism, Karl Marx and Fredrich Engels, were both in England in the 1840s and were enabled to use the plight of the working class for their own political ends. Engels came into contact with Chartism, the movement for the extension of suffrage to the workers and in 1844 wrote *Conditions of the Working Classes in England*. During this period Marx wrote a number of works, that are regarded as classical communist theory, including *Das Kapital*.

At some time, Boxhal attempted to escape the poverty by joining the 50th Regiment in the British Army. It is understandable that desperate men, made more so by hunger, could also fall in with companions of like circumstances. Resentful of the wealthy, stealing from the rich was endemic; to many it was an accepted way of life, if the opportunity presented itself. Boxhal was not immune from such influences. Somehow a very lucrative opportunity did present itself and in the company of a fellow soldier in the 50th Regiment, nineteen-year old John Jones, in the small town of Fullwood, three miles north of Preston, William Boxhal, at the age of twenty, attempted a burglary and was arrested. It was an act that dramatically changed the course of his life.

Notes:

(1) Sir Arthur Bryant, *English Saga 1840-1940*, William Collins, Fontana books, 1961 p. 74.
(2) Sir Walter Scott, *Familiar Letters*, Vol 11 19 May 1820.
(3) All the dates are taken from baptismal records which appear to be the date of baptism and are not necessarily the date of birth.
(4) Henry Mayhew and John Binny, *The Criminal Prisons of London and Scenes of Prison Life*, Frank Cass & Co Ltd., 1968 first published 1862 p. 28.
(5) Certified copy of an Entry of Death, District of Lewisham.
(6) Michael Cannon, *Who's Master? Who's Man?* Penguin Books Australia Ltd., South Yarra, 1971, pp. 42-43.

2

Convicted

The records of the Preston Quarter Session show that William Boxhal, in company with a John Jones on 23 August 1852, "At Fulwood in a shop of one Arthur Phipps Rudman did feloniously break and enter and light pieces of paper of the value of one penny ... and in the said shop ... by force of arms did steal, take and carry away sixty one pounds in money."

The partly hand written recording of the charges, on a standard printed form, is confusing, which may be the work of an incompetent clerk. It appears that the two, on the same day did also "... feloniously break and enter the shop of one George Worthington and light pieces of paper" and in what is an amazing coincidence also "... by force of arms did steal, take and carry away" exactly the same amount of money, sixty one pounds.

According to the Calender of Prisoners, at the Preston Session of October 1852 they were both found guilty of "stealing at Fullwood on 23 August, three five pound Bank of England notes, one ten pound Bank of England note, twenty four sovereigns and twelve pounds in silver, the money of George Worthington." It seems incredible that a shopkeeper would have such a vast amount of cash money on his premises and why the exact amount was said to also have been stolen from the shop of Arthur Phipps Rudman. No documents, such as the transcript of the trial can be discovered in the Lancashire Record Office in Preston.

A jury found them guilty as charged and sentenced both to be "..sent and TRANSPORTED to some part beyond the Seas for the Space of Ten Years next ..."(1)

If they did rob two places of such large sums of money, the sentence of ten year's transportation was extremely light. Earlier in the century many men and women were executed for lesser crimes. It was not until the *Offences against the Person Act 1861* that the English Parliament abolished the death penalty for all crimes other than murder and high treason.

Although sentencing was erratic, it is difficult to understand why the 10 year sentence was so low. In the same court, three months later, John Kelly and William Chambers were both convicted as pick-pockets and received sentences of transportation for 15 years (Kelly stole five shillings and sixpence); four months later, Edward Wilson recieved a 15 year sentence for having stolen a watch. (2)

In the mid-nineteenth century, it was estimated that about one-tenth of the entire English population, and one-quarter of the Irish were in need of parochial relief.(3) With many of the unemployed being without work for years and coming from a previous generation of unemployed, it was no wonder that a criminal class developed. Robbery and other types of serious felony were endemic. The middle and upper class saw their wealth threatened by the criminal poor. They imagined that a solution to the problem of wide-spread theft would be found by shipping out large numbers of convicted criminals to the colonies. The number of convicts shipped to Australia each year did not, however, greatly relieve the pressure on British jails.

The demands to solve the problem of crime were similiar to those in Australia in the 1990s, where crimes of theft, assault and burglary had increased alarmingly. Some of the causes of crime in Australia were similar to the those in nineteenth century Britain: unemployment, especially among the young, caused by Government policies of so-called "economic rationalism" and "globalisation", resulted in the collapse of the Australian manufacturing industry. There was also the serious breakdown of the Australian family. The comfortable middle class made loud demands to lock away the offenders for longer periods of imprisonment. Had there been a place to send them, there would have been a call for transportation

By the 1840s the Swan River Colony was languishing in a depression caused by a small labour-force and insufficient capital. During the first ten years since it was established in 1829 "at least half of the original British settlers left for better prospects in eastern Australia... Life in the new settlement was grim. People came close to starvation, and bad publicity in Britain ... drastically cut the supply of immigrants to Western Australia."(3a) Geography Professor Martyn Webb described the agricultural potential of the Colony as:

> The Coastal plains, at first thought to be fertile and ideally suitable
> for farming, were in reality a near desert so far as acriculture was

concerned. The settlers clung to a few urban settlements, eking out a living as best they could.

A simple but effective measure of the drastic constraints placed upon development in Western Australia by its harsh and unyielding environment is given by comparing its population growth with that of South Australia. In 1850 Western Australia's population was less than 6,000; the population of South Australia, founded seven years after the Swan River Colony was 50,000.(3b)

Desperate merchants and land-owners - conveniently for the British Government - requested the Home Office to send convicts to Western Australia. They saw the importation of cheap convict labourers as a solution to their problems, seemingly unaware that what they were demanding was a form of slave labour.

At a meeting of citizens of the Colony, held in the Perth Court house on 23 February 1849, chaired by the High Sheriff, Mr G F Stone, seven resolutions were passed. The summary of the resolutions was that because the Colony was "in a state of great depression caused by the exhaustion of the important elements of capital and labour" the call was made for "the introduction by the Home Government of persons being drafted from the various asylums in England, and men on tickets of leave."

The meeting railed on, especially, about the shortage of capital and while expressing some reservations about the "pouring in on us of felons" and that there be "an adequate guard, either of police or military to protect the colonists", decided that "a full representation of the objects of this meeting be made to His Excellency the Governor". The deputation to the Governor consisted of W Burges, AOG Lefroy, T Helms, R Habgood and G Shenton. (4)

Not all in the Colony supported the proposal and the decision did not go unchallenged. The *Perth Gazette* waged a long campaign to generate opposition to transportation. After the Home Government decided in 1849 that the Colony would become a Penal Settlement, the editor declared that it had become:

> a place wherein to cast loose the pollution of Britain, to begin a fresh career of crime and outrage upon defenceless inhabitants ... Are we to tamely and apathetically to submit to this? Truely, if we do we shall deserve the scorn and contumely of the whole world - to be pointed at with a finger of contempt as the willing companion of thieves, robbers, and murderers - as the ready introducers to our wives and families of all that is vile and infamous in humanity. (5)

The editor called for a public uprising "Let us show that...we can be united in our opposition to this tyrannous and vile breach of our privileges on the part of Earl Grey." There was no uprising or demonstration of public opposition because the majority believed that it was the only way the Colony could advance. What the editor of the *Gazette* did was to contribute to forming a public opinion of distrust of convicts and discrimination against them.

Boxhal's fate was decided by the Court in Preston; he would be sent to the Swan River Colony. It is not known whether his family knew that he had committed the offence and of his arrest; or his sentence of transportation.

Notes:

(1) For some reason there is a capitalisation of the word transported in the printed charge sheet. The details are hand written.
(2) Public Records Office, 5218 HO8, Alexander Library.
(3) Michael Cannon, *Who's Master? Who's Man?*. Penguin Books Australia Ltd., South Yarra, 1971, pp. 42-43.
(3a) Martyn Webb, "The Empire State", *The Executive State*, Constitutional Press Co. Pty Ltd., Perth, p.20. 1991.
(3b) ibid.
(4) Parliamentary Papers on Convict Dicipline and Transportation volume 1V Governor Fitzgerald to Earl Grey, 3 March, 1849.
(5) *Perth Gazette*, 30 November, 1849.

3

Incarceration

...which made England, even so recently as in the reign of the Third King George, in respect of her criminal code and her prison regulations, one of the most bloody minded and barbarous countries on the earth.

Charles Dickens (1)

When his trial was concluded and the sentence of transportation recorded, Boxhal was taken from the Preston Court, which was then in Lancaster Road. (2) He was marched, chained hand and foot, down to Church Street and then to the fortress-like Preston jail, built like a castle, and then through the twin stone towers topped, with battlements.

Behind the huge brick prison walls were several three-storey cell blocks, where he was to wait in solitary and silent confinement until arrangements were made for his assignment to another prison before transportation to Australia. Other than Gibraltar and the Bahamas, the Swan River Colony in Western Australia was the only place to which the British Government was then transporting convicts.

All convicts sentenced to be transported were numbered and described in some detail, presumably so that in the event of an escape they would be more easily identified. William Boxhal was to be numbered several times and ultimately given the number 3744. He was described as being 23 years of age; five foot eight inches tall; having light brown hair; grey eyes; a round face, with fresh complexion and being middling stout.

His occupation was that of a smith. His only identifying marks were a crown and anchor tattooed on his left arm and the letters SC on the right arm.(3) We can only speculate as to who SC was. Could it have been a first love?

It is almost certain that Boxhal was sent to Millbank Prison in London to endure what the Prison Authorities considered to be a period of punishment and "reformation". He was fortunate that he was

11

The Former Courthouse, Preston where William Boxhal was
tried and convicted (Photograph courtesy Dr. B.J.Peachey)

sentenced to be transported in 1852 because he could be moved to other jails by rail; that is if travelling, chained in an open carriage like animals - in whatever weather conditions prevailed - was fortunate. By the mid-1840s more than 4500 miles of railway lines had been laid in Britain. The railway system from Preston was connected to the Midland London line.

Twenty years earlier he and other convicts would have been made to march, manacled in heavy iron ankle and wrist cuffs and chained together, often with iron neck-pieces.

Millbank Prison was designed to accomodate the growing number of criminals in the early nineteenth century. It was completed in 1821. Located on the banks of the Thames, the buildings were described as "ugly architecture, being an ungainly combination with the mad-house and the fortress." The buildings covered an area of seven acres on sixteen acres of land. Today it is the site of the famous Tate Gallery, the National Gallery of British Art, which houses among its extensive collection the works of the great nineteenth century painter J M W Turner. It contrasts greatly with what existed in 1852.

*The Jail at Preston where William Boxhal was first imprisoned
(Photograph courtesy Dr. B.J.Peachey)*

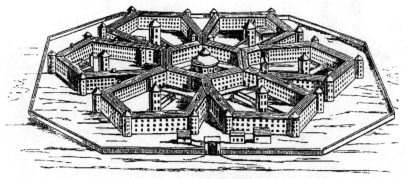

BIRD'S-EYE VIEW OF MILLBANK PRISON.
(Copied from a Model by the Clerk of the Works.)

A view of a model of Millbank Prison prepared for the Clerk of Works in 1820.
(Published by Mayhew and Binny in The Criminal Prisons of London 1862.)

The vast three-storey building, was in the shape of a hexagon consisting of six smaller buildings or a collection of prisons, in the centre of which was a chapel.

Millbank Prison was designed to be used as a receptacle for convicts under sentence or order of transportation. "They were to continue there until transported according to law ... or are directed by the Secretary of State to be removed to any other prison or place of confinement in which they may be lawfully imprisoned."(4) It was then the largest of the London prisons. At the time of Boxhal's incarceration there were 2461 male prisoners and 198 females.(5)

On arrival at the London railway terminus, Boxhal and the other prisoners assigned to Millbank would have been taken, in chains, in a prison wagon, down Parliament Street, Abington Street, along the dreary Horseferry Road, across barren ground, which was once a moat and through the Entrance lodge.

The discipline adopted in Millbank was that each convict was confined to a separate cell in which he worked and slept. The inmates were separated under the strictest seclusion, which was broke down occasionally during periods when they were made to work in the workshops - the workshops were still under the "silent system" - or on the dreaded tread-mill.

The tread-mill was a cruel device, essentially constructed to punish prisoners. It served no other purpose than punishment; the motor energy generated was rarely used for any useful purpose. The tread-mill was a long cylinder which had twentyfour steps 8 inches apart. It was operated by twelve men at a time, separated in stalls. The wheel turned twice in a minute by the men treading the steps in constant shifts of fifteen minutes.

Mayhew and Binny describe the labour of the tread-mill as excessive and quote the Government Report of the Home Inspectors of Prisons of 1838 which said that "to tread the wheel [was] an employment which is enough to make him avoid hard labour for the rest of his days".(6) It is difficult to imagine a more physically exhausting, boring, mind destroying, useless form of labour. It was indelibly etched on the mind of Oscar Wilde - even as late as 1898.

> We sewed the sacks, we broke the stones
> We turned the dusty drill:
> We banged the tins, and bawled the hymns, and sweated on the mill:
> But in the heart of every man
> Terror was lying still. (7)

Prisoners also had to learn to work at such trades as making shoes, belts, a range of garments for the military, and a large variety of other articles. Much of this work was done in the solitary confinement of their cells and in workshops where speech was forbidden. The "silent system" and solitary confinement was devised by reformers and the prison authorities to protect prisoners from contamination and aid rehabilitation. It was in effect the most severe type of punishment and would have damaged many. Charles Dickens was an opponent of the "silent system" and solitary confinement and expressed his opinions on a similar system in Philadelphia:

> I believe it, in its effects, to be cruel and wrong ...
> I hold this slow and daily tampering with the mysteries of the brain
> to be immeasurably worse than torture of the body; and because its
> ghastly signs are not so palpable to the eye and sense of touch as
> scars upon the flesh; because its wounds are not upon the surface,
> and it exhorts few cries that human ears can hear; therefore I the
> more denounce it, as a secret punishment which slumbering humanity
> is not roused up to say. (8)

The gregarious Oscar Wilde experienced the agony of solitary confinement and silence in an English jail:

A drawing of Millbank Prison from the Thames.

(Published by Mayhew and Binny in The Criminal Prisons of London 1862.)

With midnight always in one's heart,
And twilight in one's cell,
We turn the crank, or tear the rope,
Each in his seperate Hell,
And the silence is more awful far
Than the sound of a brazen bell.
Never a human voice comes near
To speak a gentle word:
And the eye that watches through the door
Is pitiless and hard:
And by all forgot, we rot and rot,
With soul and body marred.(9)

The diet at Millbank was utterly plain, but providing sustenance for ordinary labour. Breakfast consisted of 3/4 of a pint of cocoa, made of 1/2 ounce of cocoa nibs, 1/2 ounce of molasses and 2 ounces of milk and 8 ounces of bread. Dinner was 5 ounces of meat (without bone and after boiling), one pound of potatoes and 6 ounces of bread. Supper was a pint of gruel made with 2 ounces of oatmeal or wheaten flour, sweetened with 1/2 ounce of molasses and 8 ounces of bread. The punishment diet was 1 pound of bread per day and water. During 1854 four hundred and seven Millbank prisoners received the punishment diet, some in completely darkened cells. (10)

Boxhal's next move came in September 1853 when he was informed that he would be transferred to the former 74 gun ship of the line, *Defence*, converted to a prison hulk and moored in the Thames near the Woolwich Arsenal.

His move to the hulk would most likely have been done by a steam-driven cutter. It was a five-mile journey from the Millbank pier down the Thames, past the recently completed Houses of Parliament, with their great tower, then with gaping holes where the yet-to-become-famous clock faces and "Big Ben" had not been fitted.

The gracious structure that we know as Westminster Bridge had not then been built; nor had some of the other important bridges that span the Thames. It was another 30 years before the great Tower Bridge was commenced, but the mighty Tower with all its history would have been overpowering from the river. Those on board would have been awe-struck as they passed under the fine granite structure of Waterloo Bridge and the most important of all, London Bridge, with its five massive arches. When the great river wound to the north they would have seen the dome of St Paul's Cathedral on Ludgate Hill and the splendour of Christopher Wren's work. Their journey wound around the Isle of Dogs,

The workshop under the "Silent System" at Millbank Prison.
(Published by Mayhew and Binny in The Criminal Prisons of London 1862.)

through Blackwall Reach passing the Greenwich Observatory and Zero meridian longitude, and along the Greenwich Marches to Woolwich.

Such a journey would have been a delightful experience had it not been done under armed guard, chained hand and foot to other prisoners and fearful as to what would be their fate on the dreaded hulk. They may have seen, as Dickens did, when they "saw the black Hulk lying out a little way from the mud of the shore like a wicked Noah's ark, cribbed and barred and moored by massive rusty chains, the prison ship seemed ... to be ironed like the prisoners."(11)

The policy of converting old ships into prisons started at the time of the American revolution. The cessation of transportation of convicts to the American Colony in 1775 resulted in chronic overcrowding of the English prisons.

Detention in one of the damp, insanitary, rotting hulks was one of the worst forms of imprisonment in England. As Mayhew and Binny record at the time that Boxhal was interned in the *Defence* : "The hulk system condemned ... from the date of its origin to the present time, has been the despair of all penal reformers. Originally adopted as a makeshift under pressing circumstances, these old men-of-war have remained during nearly half a century, the receptacles of the worst class of prisoners from all the jails of the United Kingdom - as a striking instance of the inertness of government, as well of its utter callousness as to the fate of reformation of criminals."(12)

The dehumanising policy of solitary confinement for convicts under sentence of transportation practised at Millbank was designed, not only as a punishment, but also as a method of reformation. The segregation of offenders, who had committed minor crimes, from hardened felons, was supposed to prevent contamination. Mayhew and Binny claimed that: "Convicts who have undergone the reformatory discipline at Millbank and Pentonville are, at the hulks, suddenly brought into contact with offenders who have undergone no reformatory discipline whatever."

The move to the *Defence*, after spending nine months in solitary confinement and denied communication with others, was indeed a shock to Boxhal. Now he was thrust into close contact with some of the "worst class of prisoners".

When he arrived on the *Defence* he was given the number 1635 (13), which was attached to the back of his issue of brown and red banded convict garb. He was then directed to a ward on one of the three decks, where he was to sleep and eat with 424 other prisoners

CONVICTS FORMING A MORTAR BATTERY IN THE WOOLWICH MARSHES.

Convicts from the Defence *forming a mortar battery in the Woolwich Marshes.*
(Published by Mayhew and Binny in The Criminal Prisons of London *1862.)*

THE CONVICTS RETURNING TO THE HULKS FROM THEIR LABOUR IN THE ARSENAL.

Convicts returning to the hulks from their labour in the Arsenal..
(Published by Mayhew and Binny in The Criminal Prisons of London *1862.)*

crammed on the Hulk. This meant that at night the men slept side by side in hammocks, which were taken down each day.

Mayhew and Binny describe the sleeping wards as "a curious sight" with "a great sleeping mass of beings within them! The hammocks were slung so close to one another that they formed a perfect floor of beds on either side of the vessel. . ." Referring to the overcrowding, they go further : "The state of morality under such circumstances may be easily conceived - crimes impossible to be mentioned being commonly perpetrated"(14) Randall McGowen in commenting on the Hulks and prison reformers says that "Critics repeated tales of the immorality and violence that prevailed when the hatches were closed." (15)

The conclusion reached is that weak and vulnerable men would have been bashed and sodomised by brutish men. In such an environment, a man had to be strong enough to deter attacks. Boxhal's well documented record of good health, the muscle strength he would have developed as a blacksmith and his size could have protected him. It is interesting to note, that of the 35 prisoners from the *Defence,* who were eventually transported with Boxhal, he was taller than all but one.

Imprisonment on the Woolwich Hulks was certainly imprisonment with hard labour, and the diet was barely sustenance in the circumstances.

Each morning after muster and a breakfast of cocoa and dry bread, prisoners in groups of about 100 were taken by cutter, rowed by prisoners to the Woolwich Arsenal. Here gangs worked moving tons of soil in the marsh land or worked in the stone-yard doing the "hard, dull mechanical labour " of breaking granite. All prisoners had to "break so many bushells of stone a day according to size." There was other heavy, menial work that gangs had to perform such as carrying and cleaning shot. It was always a long unremitting nine hour day.

One of the redeeming features of the English prison system was the obligatory attendance at church services and an attempt to give some formal education to the largely illiterate inmates. This was a general policy and applied even to the Hulks. In the *Defence* a service was held in the chapel every evening, after their meal of gruel, from 6-30 to 8pm. The school was attended by groups of 55 once every 9 days and the teaching "included, reading, writing and arithmatic." The effort was wasted on some who had no desire to learn, but who preferred the class-room to hard labour. The opportunity was, however, beneficial to Boxhal.

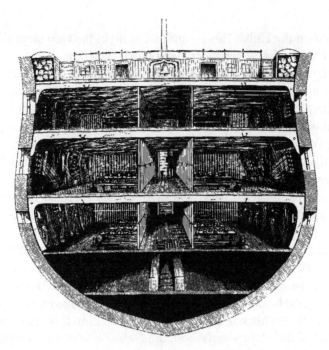

Sectional view of the interior of the Defence.
(Published by Mayhew and Binny in The Criminal Prisons of London *1862.)*

Convicts from the Defence scraping shot.
(Published by Mayhew and Binny in The Criminal Prisons of London *1862.)*

In the first week in Decenber 1855, at muster, Willian Boxhal and 34 other convicts were relieved of some of their doubts as to their future and were told that they would no longer have to labour in the Woolwich Arsenel. They were to leave the *Defence* and board the *William Hammond* at the Woolwich docks and sail for the Swan River Colony on 8 December.

The final entry regarding Boxhal, before his transfer, in the Quarterly report of the Governor of the *Defence,* stated that at the each of the preceeding 18 musters his conduct was recorded as "very good" and the surgeon reported him as "healthy". (16)

It was a motley group that accompanied him to the *William Hammond.* Most were incorrigible felons, two had life sentences and numerous others were sentenced for 15 and 20 years. But there was also the small, 17-year-old, William Perry. He was only 5 foot 2 inches tall and was sentenced for 7 years for a pick-pocket offence. (17)

An interesting group was a gang of seven who were convicted in Liverpool, on the same day in August 1854, of "armed robbery with others". All of these, would-be-highwaymen, received a 15 year sentence, except 22 year old George Allen - most likely the ring-leader, who was sentenced to 20 years. One of the group, Thomas Aspinal was to suffer greatly on the journey. The surgeon put him in the ship's hospital when they boarded the *William Hammond* on 6 December.

Notes:

(1) Charles Dickens, *American Notes and Pictures of Italy*, Chapman and Hall Ltd. and Humphrey Milford, New York: Oxford University Press American Branch, p.63.

(2) The Courthouse used at the time of Boxhal's trial is now the County and Regimental Museum.

(3) Convict list, *William Hamond*, Battye Library.

(4) The First Report of the Millbank Prison, 31 July, 1842, as quoted by H. Mayhew and J. Binney p. 236.

(5) H.Mayhew and J. Binny, *The Criminal Prisons of London,* Frank Cass and Co London 1968, first published 1862, p.238.

(6) ibid., p.305.

(7) Oscar Wilde, "The Ballad of Reading Gaol". *The Complete Works of Oscar Wilde.* Hamlyn Publishing Group Ltd London, 1983, p.731.
This poem is the most powerful of all Wilde's poems. It was published in 1898, soon after Wilde's release from prison, many years after Boxhal's imprisoment. It describes the torments of silence, the tread-mill, the harshness and the starkness of prison life, even after the prison reforms of the late nineteenth century.

(8) Charles Dickens, op. cit., p.111.

(9) Oscar Wilde, op. cit. p.741.

(10) Mayhew and Binny, op. cit., pp. 255-9.
(11) Charles Dickens,*Great Expectations,* facsimile reproduction edition, Marshal Cavendish Ltd., 1986, p.38.
(12) Mayhew and Binney, op. cit., pp., 201-2.
(13) Public Records Office, 5215 HO 8/118, Alexander Library.
(14) Mayhew and Binny, op. cit., pp., 199 - 209.
(15) N. Morris and D.J. Rothman eds., *The Oxford History of the Prison,* Oxford University Press, New York, 1998, p.76.
(16) Public Records Office, 5215 HO 8/126, Alexander Library.
(17) ibid 5219.

4

Transported

From distant climes, o'er widespread seas we come,
(Though not with much eclat, or beat of drum)
True patriots all; for be it understood,
We left our country for our country's good.

William Boxhal and the 34 other convicts were taken in batches in a
gig rowed by four other convicts from the *Defence,* a short distance to
the barque, *William Hammond,* moored at the Woolwich docks. They
assembled on deck for the customary roll call and were allocated
numbers, given a set of clothes for the journey and directed by a guard
through the low hatch to a bunk in one of the prison holds. The allocation
of numbers to the convicts from the *Defence* is interesting. Boxhal and
John King who had very good conduct records were given low numbers
3744 and 3745 respectively and the other 33 were placed last in the
series of numbers running consecutively from 3939. Unlike Boxhal
and King, none of the latter were given a ticket-of-leave until months,
and in some instances, years after their arrival, which is an indication
of their standing with the prison authorities.

It is probable that there would have been relatives and friends of
some of the convicts on the cold and miserable dock to bid them a sad
farewell as they left their homeland, almost certainly for ever. Although
Woolwich is only about 2 miles from the last known places, Deptford
and Lewisham, where the Boxhal family had lived, there is no evidence
that either his mother or his brothers and sisters came to say goodbye.

In the depth of a London winter on 8 December 1855, the *William
Hammond,* under the command of Captain Horatio Edwards, was towed
by a steam tug from the Woolwich dock to mid-stream on an outgoing
tide and sailed down the Thames. It had taken on a further 32 convicts
from the Hulk *Warrior.*

When the ship cleared the Straits of Dover and entered the English
Channel it encounted "very heavy gales and cold weather" (1). The
pitching and rolling and the pounding of wind and sea, would have

been a terrifying experience for the convicts in the dark unfamiliar prison hold, fouled by seasick men, many of whom may have never been on a ship.

The *William Hammond* then proceeded along the south coast of England to Portsmouth, where on 17 December it took on another 58 convicts. The following day it anchored off the Isle of Portland, which AG Evans describes more accurately as a peninsular. "[it] is a wild and precipitous headland rising 150 metres above the sea, thrusting out into the English Channel from the Dorset coast 13 kilometres distant. The headland or 'Bill', is joined to the mainland by a narrow ridge of shingle, Chesil Bank. Rising from the sea like a sleeping giant, Portland Bill presents an awsome barrier to vessels plying up and down the English Channel...[it] makes an ideal site for a prison, being inaccessible from the sea and approachable only by way of Chesil Bank." (2)

A further 80 prisoners in convict garb, were marched, chained by hand and leg from the prison to board a waiting steam driven boat which took them out to the *William Hammond*. Once on board and their details recorded, they were put through the narrow hatch to the prison hold and allocated a bunk which would be their space for the next three months.

The dehumanising, forced silence of prison life was now broken and there was no restriction on a prisoner talking to the man next to him. Few if any of the prisoners knew the man next to him or any others in the hold. It was difficult for some to communicate after the constraints of long periods of imposed silence and there was a natural inclination to be careful. The prison contained a conglomeration of hardened, cruel men and also the relatively innocent; some were unprincipled criminals and others were petty thieves who were inveigled into crime because it was the thing to do; others had stolen because they and their families were hungry.

Boxhal seems to have had an intelligent and determined intention to rise above the degrading brutality of his incarceration. To do this while in the company of incorrigible felons, some of whom were intrinsically bad, required a mind set and a kind of prophetic or sanguine understanding of what lay ahead in Australia. His behaviour in Millbank and on the *Defence* must have been exemplary, because of the report that was made on his character.

The *William Hammond* lay anchored off Portland for several days before leaving on the morning of Christmas Eve, 1855. Once under sail in quiet seas the prisoners were allowed on deck, where they experienced their first diversion. A seaman, John Gollately, fell

(O)

OFFICIAL LOG BOOK. No. 4.

FOR

EITHER FOREIGN GOING OR HOME TRADE SHIP.

Name of Ship.	Official Number.	Port of Registry.	Registered Tonnage.	Name of Master.	No. of his Certificate (if any).
W. Hammond	5113	London	685	Hector Edward	5113

Date of Commencement of the Voyage _December 7th 1855_

Nature of the Voyage or Employment _Australia & India_

Delivered to the Shipping Master of the Port of _London Holloy_ the _5th_

day of _December_ 1856.

Signed _George Dunlop_

Shipping Master.

NOTE.—The above Entries are to be filled up by the Master, and the Log Book is to be delivered to the Shipping Master within forty-eight hours after the Ship's arrival, or upon the discharge of the Crew, whichever first happens, in the case of a "Foreign-going Ship;" and within twenty-one days after the 30th of June and the 31st of December respectively in every year in the case of a "Home Trade Ship."—*See* 286.

LONDON:
PRINTED BY GEORGE EDWARD EYRE AND WILLIAM SPOTTISWOODE,
PRINTERS TO THE QUEEN'S MOST EXCELLENT MAJESTY.

1855.

Cover sheet of the Official Log Book of the William Hammond.

overboard and much to the delight and entertainment of the convicts, a seaman attacked the Chief Mate. Captain Edwards records the incident in the log:

> At 9am off Portland Chief Mate sent five seamen out to bestow the jib when a seaman by the name of John Gollately fell overboard. We succeeded in picking him up with a rope on the starboard quarter. Just at the time the man was got on board a seaman by the name of John Deady struck the Chief Mate a blow saying it was his fault the man fell overboard for sending them out to stow the jib. The Master interposed and stopped the man from striking the Mate again. The then Mate made use of a great deal of talk saying he would be his bitter enemy for all the voyage. This all occurred on the poop causing great disorder in the ship many convicts being on deck at the time, that the Surgeon Superintendent thought it necessary to call out the guard. After a little time order was again made and the Master ordered hands out to stow the jib which was done without any further trouble.(3)

The seaman, John Deady was spoken to by the Captain but "was in no way sorry for what he had done." The poor fellow was tried before a Magistrate in Plymouth on 1 January and "sentenced to 21 days imprisonment for an assault on the Chief Mate."

The *William Hammond* left England from Plymouth on 5 January 1856; leaving behind six seamen, who, because of "several diseases and ruptures" were deemed to be unfit to travel. It took on board a further 45 prisoners from Dartmoor. The cargo of humanity was wretched. Seasickness alone, apart from any other maladies, would have rendered the dark, cold, crowded hold a revolting mess.

The official policy of the English Government was that convicts ships should not be embarked during the depth of winter. Most probably, because of sheer inefficiency and bureacratic bungling and the commercial consequences to and the pressure from the shipping contractors, this policy was ignored in the case of the *William Hammond* and some other ships. Permitting convicts to suffer intense cold in the dank prison hold of a ship was callously cruel.

It is remarkable that only one person died on the journey, which may be due to the diligence of the Surgeon-superintendent, Dr George MacLaren, who in his report does appear to claim credit for the survival of those on board. The unfortunate man who died was a Corporal in the Pensioner Guard, 47-year-old Henry Fraser, "who was discharged from the army in 1845 for "General Debility" came on board in an emaciated state, having recently been discharged from the Military

Hospital at Plymouth, where he had been for some months for a disease of the chest." The surgeon diagnosed him as having "Phthisis Pulmonalis", which was almost certainly tuberculous. He spent much time in the ship's hospital and died two weeks before reaching the destination at 4.30am on 13 March.(4)

The planned journey was to sail directly to Fremantle. Many ships would have stopped at Cape Town or Rio de Janeiro to replenish supplies. Presumably the direct route was a bureaucratic decision to avoid the possiblity of an attempted escape of the convicts. It would also have been less costly to the ship owners, which is more likely to have been the motivation for the direct passage. This meant, however, that valuable space was taken up with food and water.

The *William Hammond* was a new ship, built in the famous shipyards at Sunderland in 1853 for Thomas and Co. It may well have been been designed and equipped for the transportation of convicts, at the time of construction, with sufficient bunks and some water closets. It was clasified A1 in 1855 and would have been superior and also dryer than some of the smaller rotting vessels that transported convicts to New South Wales and Van Dieman's Land in earlier times.

Nevertheless it was a relatively small ship of only 683 tons. To envisage what the conditions for the convicts would have been like, it is necessary to know the size of the ship and the number it carried. It was 149.5 feet long, 28.6 feet wide and had a depth of 19 feet. Crowded on board were 250 convicts; in the "steerage" there were 30 Pensioner Guards, 20 women and 40 children. The crew numbered 32 and there were 8 cabin passengers. Including the Captain and the Surgeon-superintendent, Dr George MacLaren, there was a total of 382 persons.

Assuming that there were two levels below deck and allowing for a bilge and the thickness of timbers, each level would have had a height of no more than six feet. This would have given some headroom, because most were short in stature. The tallest man was 5 foot 11inches.

To say living conditions were cramped would have been an understatement. The arrangements for the security of convicts would not have differed from most other convict ships. As Charles Bateson describes the typical convict ship: "The 'tween deck was divided into four large sections, with a heavy oak bulkhead running from side to side where the mast came through the deck. The space forward of the bulkhead was reserved for the prisoners, whose sole means of entry or egress was through a small iron-studded door in the bulkhead. It would allow the passage of one man at a time, and to pass through it he had to stoop and almost crawl. The hospital was situated on the starboard side abaft the bulkhead, with corresponding space on the port side serving as quarters of the warders and their families ... Then came the crew's quarters, with the guard and their families quartered aft." (5)

In the foward section there would have been a chain locker and space to stow anchors, spare rope, sails and paint. Much space would have been taken up with a galley and access to an area for the storage of food and water. Assuming that each person consumed on average as little as a kilogram of food and a litre of water each day, meant that, allowing for spoilage, the ship had to carry more than 40 tonnes of bulky food, including fresh fruit and barrels of wine and 30,000 litres of water. Water would have been replenished at times by rain and it was a common practice for such ships to catch fish and even sea birds.

With bulkheads seperating various types of prisoners the 250 convicts would have been confined to an area of about 300 square metres. Each convict had the shared confined space of 1.2 square metres for the three months of the journey. Allowing for an area in which the convicts ate and water closets for the disposal of excrement, the double bunks may well have been no more the half a metre wide with half a metre between each pair.

Dr MacLaren reports on his demand for cleanliness because the convicts "were huddled together in a small depressed [space] and agitated by a variety of conflicting influences inseparable from convicted criminals on their way to a penal settlement." (5) What seems to be implied here is what was common on convict ships: that there were physical and sexual assaults by brutish men.

The best known of West Australian convicts, the Fenian, John Boyle O'Reilly, was transported to Western Australia on the last convict ship, the *Hougoumont,* in 1867, and later escaped to America. In his novel, *Moondyne Joe* he describes how the convicts would have suffered:

> The first few days of the voyage are inexpressibly horrible. The hundreds of pent-up wretches are unused to the darkness of the ship, strange to their crowded quarters and to each other, depressed in spirits at their endless seperation from home, sickened to death with the merciless pitch and roll of the vessel, alarmed at the dreadful thunder of the waves against their prison walls and fearful of the sudden engulfment with the hatches barred. The scene is too hideous for a picture - too dreadful to be described in words.
> Only those who have stood within the bars, and heard the din of devils and the appalling sounds of dispair, blended in a diapason that made every hatch-mouth a vent of hell can imagine the horrors of the hold of a convict ship.(6)

At that time of the year, rough weather could have been encounted for the first two weeks until they reached the Madeira and Canary islands at about 30 degrees latitude north. With calmer weather the convicts would have been mustered on deck with their bedding to be aired.

Their first sighting of land would have been about 6 February when they passed to the west of the mountains of Cape Verde Islands. It is likely that the convicts would have been permitted to spend time on deck as they passed the great volcano, Pico do Cano rising more than 9000 feet from the Island of Fogo.

Boxhal is not recorded as having suffered from any complaint or having received any treatment, but Dr MacLaren reports cases of dysentery, diarrhoea and disease of the chest. "There were also serious problems for the convicts, confined for long periods in the dark prison hold when allowed on deck." As Dr Maclaren records, there were cases of "nyetalophia [where] the retina was no doubt in a state of impaired sensibility, arising from exposure to the brilliant light of day...in consequence of the sudden transmissions to which the prisoners were necessarily subjected to in passing from obscure light to the glare of the upper deck."(7)

In the weeks that followed as the ship neared the equator they would have suffered even more from the intense heat. None would ever have experienced temperatures in the region of 40 degrees celsius, and quickly passing from near freezing to such unaccustomed temperatures would have been difficult to bear. If allowed on deck, the intense direct rays of the sun would have caused harm to many. During the frequent times when the ship was becalmed in equatorial waters the prison hold would have seemed like a stinking Hell-hole.

John Boyle O'Reilly recounts the conditions on the convict ship when it wallowed in burning heat:

> When the ship was becalmed in the tropics, the suffering of the imprisoned wretches in the steaming and crowded hold was piteous to see. They were so packed that free movement was impossible. The best thing to do was to sit each on his berth and suffer in patience.
>
> The air was stifling and oppressive. There was no draught through the barred hatches. The deck above them was blazing hot. The pitch dropped from the seams and burned their flesh as it fell.
>
> There was only one word spoken or thought - one yearning idea in every mind - water, cool water to slake the parching thirst.
>
> Two pints of water a day was served out to each convict - a quart of putrid and blood warm liquid. It was woful (sic) to see the thirsty soul devour this allowance as soon as their hot hands seized the vessel.

Day in and day out, the terrible calm held the ship and the
consuming heat sapped the lives of the pent-up convicts.(8)

O'Reilly's work is fiction, but what he described could probably
have been the situation on the *Hougoumount*. It may have been worse
on the *William Hammond*, which sailed eleven years earlier. The
Hougoumont was a much larger ship than the *William Hammond*, being
192 tons heavier and 28 feet longer, but it carried only 30 more convicts.

The Chief Mate, Mr David Kid, found himself in deep trouble again
when they approached the tropics. On 28 January Captain Edwards
records that:

> At 8pm Master and Surgeon was taking their usual round to see all
> well. On going down the afte hold master observed that the afte
> store hatch was not locked, and on asking the Third Mate or store
> keeper he was told that Mr Kid, Chief Mate had been down there for
> business which did appear to him to be feasable as it was his
> watching. It was shortly afterward that Mr Kid, Chief Mate was
> intoxicated and quarrelsome about the deck. At 10.30 pm Master
> went in Poop and found him asleep on his watch on deck, which
> caused the master to step on deck until 12 o'clock, the Second and
> Third Mates was then called and on coming on deck the Chief Mate
> was still asleep. Their attention was called to the circumstances by
> the Master, he then went below leaving the Second Mate in charge
> with orders to call him again at 4 o'clock. On his coming up at 4
> o'clock was informed by the Second Officer that Mr Kid had slept
> in the same place until 2 o'clock and then got up and went to his bed
> without saying anything. He was called again at 4 o'clock and came
> on deck. At 6 he spoke to the Master and said he was sorry for what
> had occured and promised that it would it should not be the case
> again, but the master knew that it was not the first time it had occurred
> and he could not look over it, requesting him to give up the key of
> the store room that he had charge of as it was quite clear it was
> Government Stores he was making use of that he could go on with
> his duty but that he must leave the ship on her arrival at Swan River
> and that he was liable to severe punishment for such conduct and to
> have his Certificate of Competancy taken from him. This was read
> to him in the Cuddy.(9)

Captain Edwards may have reconsidered his decision to leave Mr
Kid at Swan River, or Kid may have become a reformed character
during the balance of the journey, because there is no record of him
remaining in the Colony.

The *William Hammond* would have drawn level with the Cape of
Good Hope by about 19 February and then travelled 1000 miles south

In the "roaring forties" By Murray McDonald.

to about latitude fortyfive degrees or lower to catch the trade winds or "roaring forties" and shorten the actual distance travelled. The temperature again dropped to near freezing, day and night; this combined with the might of the wind confined the convicts for long periods to the misery of the prison hold, with the fearful pounding and the constant pitching and rolling. The Surgeon-Superintendent reported that "... getting into the cool weather, south of the line a few cases of colarch and rheumatism appeared."

As they drew near the coast of Western Australia, sailing north- west to reach the 32nd latitude, the temperature rose and the wind abated. More time was spent on deck in the pleasant mild autumn sun. With the knowledge that their journey was coming to an end there was a growing sense of hope and expectation. Excitement increased as the crew brought anchors on deck, checked the long boat and worked to prepare the ship for landing. At seven in the evening of 28 March the lighthouse on Rottnest Island was sighted, with the cry of "land ho" causing great excitement to those on deck. The news spread quickly to the steerage passengers, the guards and to the convicts in the prison hold.

In the early morning, in the lee of Rottnest Island, the sound of the anchors rattling out and thudding into the shallow waters of the roads off Fremantle, and the stillness of the ship, brought a feeling of relief to the prisoners. Their miserable journey had ended.

The *William Hammond* was boarded by the Harbour Master the following morning at 7am on what was most likely a typical, still, sun-bright autumn day, that few if any on board had experienced or expected. Ports and hatches were opened to allow the convicts to gaze at their new home. They could see a roundish building on a headland, which appeared like a fort, but was later revealed to be a prison. There were white cottages at the opening to the Swan River and several larger buildings; one a long four-story, seemingly grand structure on higher ground. This they were later to discover was the Fremantle Prison, called the "Establishment". It had recently been built by convicts for convicts and the inmates of the *William Hammond* would be incarcerated in it when they disembarked. A clear sky and a brilliant blue sea, which broke onto a long stretch of white beach with a backdrop of hills to the east was a dramatic contrast to their recollections of the cold, overcast, filthy towns of England.

By mid-afternoon on 29 March the cabin passengers and the families of the pensioner guards disembarked with their possessions by lighter and long-boat to Fremantle.

The convicts had to wait for two days before the last of them left the ship. Tom Aspinel, one of the Liverpool gang of highwaymen, who had suffered greatly throughout the journey from phthisis was the first to be taken off at 2pm on 1 April. He was sent to the Fremantle Hospital and died 24 days later.

With the exception of those who had been recalcitrant during the voyage, it was the first time since leaving England that they were put in leg-irons and chained together. The climb down into the lighter was difficult as was their climbing out onto the deep water jetty at the southern end of Cliff Street on arrival.

As each batch arrived they were marched through the white sandy streets of Fremantle under the gaze of the citizens, some hoping to recognise a friend or relative from England. It was a dishevelled, forlorn group of humanity, wearing dirty prison garb, that shuffled in clanking chains, the mile or so to the large, white limestone-walled Fremantle prison.

Notes:

(1) Report of the Surgeon-superintendent, Dr George MacLaren.
(2) A.G. Evans, *Fanatic Heart. A life of John Boyle O'Rielly*, University of Western Australia Press, Nedlands, 1997, p.54.
(3) Log of Captain Horatio Edwards.
(4) Report of the Surgeon-superintendent, Dr George MacLaren.
(5) Charles Bateson, *The Convict Ships 1787-1868*, A.H. & A.W. Reed, 1974, Sydney, p. 303.
(6) John Boyle O'Reilly, *Moondyne Joe,* P.J.Kenedy & Sons New York, p. 208.
(7) Report of the Surgeon-superintendent, Dr George MacLaren.
(8) John Boyle O'Reilly, *Moondyne Joe*, opcit., pp. 230-231.
(9) Log of Captain Horatio Edwards.

5

Ticket of Leave

When the convicts arrived at the prison, they experienced the luxury of a hot bath in the ablution block and were given a hair-cut and beard trim. Their details were once again painstakingly recorded in a journal and they were given a medical examination and marched to the cells. The quiet stillness of the small narrow cell and the lack of motion was a strange sensation in the hammock during their first night.

At a muster during the first week of April, 1856, William Boxhal and 51 other convicts were separated from the others and informed that they were to be given a ticket-of-leave. The prison officer handed each a parchment certificate and spelled out his rights and obligations. Boxhal was able to be employed by the free settlers and merchants in the Colony or by the Government and would be paid a wage at the going rate but he would be under the supervision of the police and could be arrested at any time if he committed any trivial offence; he must not consume any alcohol; he must report regularly to the authorities and he would have to get a travelling pass if he wished to leave the district in which he was to reside. They were then given a set of non-convict clothes.

William Boxhal would have felt a mixture of relief and elation. He was to be a free man! The rigours of prison life were over. This was the turning-point in his life. He had withstood the suffering of the past three and a half years and had survived; he was only 24 years of age and would work and be successful in this new land. The constraints of the ticket-of-leave were of little concern; he would obey the rules. He had been handed a jewell of great price - his freedom.

It may have been fortunate that the ticket-of-leave men had arrived during the time when Captain A. E. Kennedy was Governor of the Colony. Unlike Dr J. S. Hampton, who had previously been Comptroller General of convicts in Van Dieman's land, who succeeded him in 1862, Kennedy had a reputation for a more humane, lenient treatment of the convicts. Likewise the Comptroller General in charge of convicts,

Captain E Y Henderson was a man with a similar reputation. It may have been Governor Kennedy's lenient attitude, but more likely a report of good behaviour (1), and that he had served more than three years of his sentence, that led to William Boxhal and the 51 other prisoners being given their ticket-of-leave on arrival.

The morning they were to leave the Fremantle prison, they were roused at 4 am; after roll-call and breakfast, the ticket-of-leave men were marched in batches to the town jetty in the river at the northern end of Cliff Street, there to board a boat to be taken to the town of Perth.

The wide heavy clinker-built whaler had a crew of three, a forward hand, one who handled the main-sheet and a man in charge at the tiller. They were instructed to stow their baggage fore and aft and to sit on the plank seats. Those who sat near the boom were advised that they may be told to duck their heads when the boat went about, which only happened twice on the journey.

By late morning the westerly breeze had freshened and the craft, despite its wide beam and heavy load, moved easily out into mid-stream, running up the river with the wind. For William Boxhal and his fellow ticket-of-leave men, who had only three months earlier left behind the dampness of England in mid-winter, its penertrating cold, drizzle and fog, and buildings stained black by centuries of pollution, this new country was a dramatic contrast in almost every respect. The brilliant sunshine reflecting off the white sand, hurting the eyes; the seemingly endless clear blue skies; long yellow grass, burnt dry at the end of a hot summer and the strange harsh green of the trees and low scrub, aroused curiosity and amazement.

They were enthralled by the beauty of the river. The journey commenced past tall lime-stone cliffs with white sand at the water's edge, teaming with abundant bird life. They were especially fascinated by the numerous black swans, after which the river was named. Big lumbering, white pelicans with the enormous beak, ran across the water and launched into graceful flight.

The limestone cliffs gradually receded and flatter land appeared. The boat had to skirt a long sand bar that stretched from the eastern shore, bringing them close to the west bank of the river. Now they were able to see more closely the vegetation that was so new to them; tall eucalyptus trees, lower banksia and the unique black trunked, grass-topped 'Blackboys'.

There was also the occasional house, with English-styled gardens and recognisable fruit trees. Such developments were reassuring to these slightly shocked immigrants in a strange land. There was great excitement at the first sighting of a kangaroo and also of the black Aborigines, who occasionally watched from the bank.

Beautiful as the river was, they were not prepared for their entry into the three-mile-wide expanse of water where the Canning River joined the Swan. There were some who said that it was no longer the river, perhaps a lake or even the ocean. Soon they could see the buildings of Perth and to the west a hill which came down to the edge of the river. They could have been told by the man on the tiller that they were still on the river and the hill was called Mount Eliza.

The hill seemed to shelter the river from the wind, but the whaler glided gently to a long jetty where a group of people waited. Once again there was the unorganised disembarking and the reporting to officials.

Perth was a larger town with more people than Fremantle. It was also the seat of government and the centre of the commercial life of the colony. In the orderly well-laid-out streets there were more and bigger buildings than in Fremantle; some were made of brick and many more were under construction, which indicated employment opportunities for the mainly labouring-class arrivals. In the wide and dusty main thoroughfare, Saint George's Terrace, which ran parallel to the river, there were numerous houses and many fine buildings, such as, the Saint George's Church, across the road from the Governor's residence and the court house. To the Western end was Perth Boys' School; it looked like a church, built in a Gothic style, with a high-pitched shingled roof that supported a bell-tower with a cross on top.

The first night in Perth would have been spent at the Convict Depot. The 52 would have been allocated into groups for dispatch to the several regional Convict Depots, where they would be employed by settlers or used by the Government on much needed road works. The latter was least desired by the ticket-of-leave men. It was usually harder, more disciplined work and gave them less freedom.

They were awakened at 5 am on the morning of their departure. After parade and roll-call, prayers and a breakfast of bread, treacle and sweet tea, they stowed their gear on horse-drawn wagons, destined for various country Convict Depots. There are no records as to which Depot William Boxhal was sent or who was his first employer. We do know, however, he was employed by Bishop Salvado as a shepherd at the Benedictine Mission at New Norcia in 1858 (3); when he first purchased land he gave his address as Victoria Plains; when he married in 1863 it was Victoria Plains-Toodyay, therefore it is reasonable to assume that he was sent to the Depot at Toodyay, which was established in August, 1851.

The usual method of transferring convicts and ticket-of-leave men to the various depots was for them to march with a guard beside a wagon. Depending on the size of the party, the load on the wagon and the fitness of the men, it was unlikely that they could ride. Provisions for five days were carried, but barring mishaps and bad weather, the 60 mile journey could sometimes be done in three days.

The party set off on the journey along St George's Terrace, past the Governor's residence and some substantial houses. Once again they marvelled at the expanse of the wide blue river that they could see from the road as they approached the causeway, a series of wooden bridges built in 1842, that spanned the Swan River, stretching about a mile across the Heirisson Island flats. They then proceeded north to Guildford, where they would most probably have spent the first night at the Convict Depot in Meadows Street.

About five kilometres out of Guildford the road forked, one road going to York, the other up what was then known as "Toodyay Greenmount", but today has the name of "Red Hill". This required a slow climb up into the Darling Range on a steep, rough rocky track. The view across the coastal plain to the ocean and stretching north and south as far as the eye could see was spectacular and gave them an impression of the vastness of the country they had come to.

The party would have spent their first night out of Guildford at a road station, set up to house convicts who maintained the road. Lieutenant Du Cane, the officer in charge of the Guildford Convict Depot in 1854, reported:

> On the Toodyay Road about six miles from hence, a station has been erected capable of containing 60 men, a room for the sick, a cooking house, a warder's quarters, and a quarter and store room for the assistant superintendent; these buildings are of mud, with thatched roofs, the timber in the vicinity not being so well adapted as to make slab houses as on the York Road. (4)

The next morning the usual procedure of roll-call, prayers and breakfast followed before leaving the road station. The journey then proceeded through stands of jarrah and white gum. It is possible that the party would have had their first meal of kangaroo. The shooting of this strange animal by the guard, skinning and quartering, it would have been an exciting diversion in the long slow march. The smell of the fire used for roasting parts of it, started with eucalyptus leaves and blackboy, was a new and pleasing sensation. The next two nights the men would have slept in the open under a canopy of the brightest stars; another new experience for Englishmen, with memories of dull overcast skies and fog. It was also a taste of what would become common place for those who would be employed as shepherds, spending long periods in bush camps.

Their reaction as they approached the small town of Toodyay in the fertile Avon valley may well have been similiar to those who first discovered the area in 1831. George Fletcher Moore, who was one of that party recorded: "... we suddenly found ourselves on a promontory, abruptly sinking into a large and beautiful valley. This view elevated our spirits again; "Worcestershire" cried one; "Shropshire" cried another; "Kilkenny for ever," roared Sheriden." (5) But when Boxhal and the men entered the valley that had been settled for almost twenty years the scene was different; mud brick cottages and some commercial buildings sparsley lined the main street. The tall grass was dry after a long hot summer, but the fruit trees and various deciduous English trees were a welcome blaze of familiar autumn red and yellow. The road followed the then pooled upper reaches of the Swan River, which in late winter would become a wide fast-running flooded expanse of water. The early settlers had given this part of the river the name Avon, because nostalgia reminded them of places like Worcestershire where flows the Avon.

They would have been billeted at the Convict Depot at the eastern end of the town to await to be offered employment. It is possible William Boxhal may have stayed in Toodyay, but more likely that he was employed by a pastoralist in the Victoria Plains.

Notes:
(1) J.S. Battye Library, acc 128.
(2) E. K. Crowley, *Australia's Western Third,* Macmillan & Co., London, 1960, p.34.
(3) New Norcia records, Acc., 2953A/24, p.16.
(4) Lieutenant Du Cane, Report of works from Guildford, Vol. V11 p. 148.
(5) G. F. Moore, *Diary of Ten Years of an Early Settler in Western Australia,* University of Western Australia Press, Nedlands, 1978, p.79.

6

Victoria Plains

Victoria Plains was a loosely-defined area, which included New Norcia, Bindoon, Bolgart, Toodyay and as far north as Moora. Captain John Scully, the Resident Magistrate in Toodyay, named it after Queen Victoria.

Parts of the area were first sought as pastoral leases in the early 1840s by Captain John Scully, who explored some of the Moore River and had a property at Bolgart Springs. There were other early settlers, such as the Drummonds and the Macphersons, who grazed flocks of sheep even before the leases were granted.

The development of the area received a boost in 1846 with the arrival in the Colony of a small community of Benedictine missionaries led by two Spaniards, Dom Joseph Benedict Serra and Dom Rosendo Salvado. They were part of a group of priests, nuns and catechists brought to the Colony by Bishop Brady. The party arrived on the *Elizabeth*, after a 113 day journey, on 7 January 1846.

Captain Scully, who was related to one of the Sisters of Mercy Nuns, persuaded the Benedictines to set up a mission in the Victoria Plains, "where aborigines were numerous" and offered to cart their goods.

During the intense heat of February they walked the rugged track up the Darling scarp to Toodyay, then onto Scully's property at Bolgart where they rested for three days before travelling on to a an area near the Moore River, the local aborigines called Noondagoonda. Here they built a crude bush hut for shelter. After months of hardship, near starvation and with no knowledge of leasing land, they were forced to abandon their hut because it was on land leased by the scottish shepherds, Mackintosh and Macpherson. They moved to a piece of unoccupied land at Maurin Pool. Wiser now, they acquired twenty acres of freehold land, the beginning of their permanent mission. They named the place New Norcia after Norcia in Italy, the birthplace of St Benedict.

Salvado was 32 years of age when he arrived in the Colony. He was a cultured, scholarly man, a talented musician and endowed with

*Bishop Rosendo Salvado OSB. Pastoralist and benefactor
and evangelist to the aborigines and the pioneers.
(Photograph courtesy Benedictine Community at New Norcia).*

physical strength and stamina. But his greatest characteristic was his unselfish dedication to better the lives of the aborigines. He worked with great faith and intelligent perseverance, despite, as he wrote: "When we penetrated into the thick bush in February 1846 we found only creatures who were more bestial than human: natives who killed and ate each other... husbands who killed their wives over some trifling matter; mothers who put their third girl-child to death, giving as their only reason that there were too many females already..." (1)

Whilst in Rome seeking financial support for the Church, Salvado was consecrated Bishop of the Diocese of Port Victoria (formerly Port Essington) in the Northern Territory on 15 August 1849.(2) The small settlement at Port Essington on the Cobourg Peninsular, north-east of where Darwin is today, was soon abandoned. Salvado never exercised his episcopal role in the nonexistent Diocese.

A decree from Rome on 1 April 1859 proclaimed the New Norcia Mission independent of Perth and gave Salvado authority over it -a position he held with distinction for fifty years-. Few had such a profound impact on the Colony in the second half of the nineteenth century than Salvado. He also had a profound effect on the life of William Boxhal and other former convicts.

By the time Boxhal came to the area, there were several well established and relatively wealthy pastoralists, like A O'G Lefroy at "Walebing", James Clinch at "Berkshire Valley" and the Irish families of Butlers and Clunes.

It is probable that he could have been employed by Clinch and Butler or some other pastoralists, but more likely by Dom Salvado. Although there is no record of Boxhall having worked at New Norcia before 1858, the surviving monastery records show him as having entered into a contract with Bishop Salvado on 8 January 1858, twenty months after he was granted his ticket-of-leave. The scrupulously kept hand-written agreement reads:

> *I the undersigned do hereby agree with his Lordship Bp Salvado to take charge of a flock of sheep as a shepherd from this day at a rate of 50/- per month on the first six months and at the rate of 60/- per month the other six months and my weekly provisions as follows*
> *Meat 12 lb*
> *Flour 14 lb*
> *Sugar 1 1/2 lb*
> *Tea 4 oz*
> *Bran 7 lb for one only dog*
> *I bound myself to obey the overseer's orders as those of his Lordship*

I the undersigned do hereby agree with His Lordship Bp Salvado to take charge of a flock of sheep as Shepherd for twelve Kalendar Months from this day at the rate of 50/ per month on the first six months and at the rate of 60/ per month the other six months, and my weekly provisions as follows

Meat 12 ℔
Flour 14 "
Sugar 1½ "
Tea — 4 ounces
Bran 7 ℔ for one only dog

I bound myself to obey the overseer's orders as those of His Lordship himself and moreover of keeping the sheep clean and in the best possible order —

New Norcia 8th January 1858

William Boxhall

William Boxhal's first contract of employment with Bishop Salvado 8 January 1858. (Acc 2953A/5 Benedictine Archives New Norcia).

self and moreover of keeping the sheep clean and in best possible order.

New Norcia 8 January 1858

Signed William Boxhall (3)

The pay of 50 and 60 shillings a month was more than double what the Mission paid to some shepherds, recorded in the same journal. This seems to indicate that his reliability and the quality of his work was highly regarded and that he must have worked for the Mission or near to it before the contract was drawn up. On 31 December 1858 Boxhal is recorded as being in charge of 796 sheep; 13 had died, he had lost 11 and 7 were killed for his own use. (4)

Another former convict, Charles Delaney had numerous contracts with the Mission, doing well-digging, land-clearing, timber- splitting and fence construction. Delaney was Irish and had been a soldier in the British army in Bombay. He was found guilty of a "Martial breach of Articles of War" and sentenced to 14 years' transportation. He arrived in the colony on the *General Godwin* on 28 March 1854 and received his ticket-of-leave about the same time as Boxhal on 17 April, 1856.(5) They may well have been in the same group at the Toodyay Convict Depot when first employed.

Delaney and Boxhal entered into a formal partnership on 2 May 1862 and contracted with Bishop Salvado to cut and errect post and rail fencing. The contract stated that the work was to be done

> *at the rate ten shillings and six pence per chain. The rail shall be nine feet long, the posts six feet six inches long, out of the ground, five feet and eighteen inches under the ground. The whole fence shall be splitted timber, sound, substantial and strong, three rail fence put up also in a workman like manner." (6)*

The location was not specified.

The work was hard manual labour. The timber logs would have been carried from the mission stockpile. Because there is no mention of tools in the contract - which was common in the mission contracts - they would have had to use their own axes, adzes, shovels, wedges and sledge hammers. A chain of fencing required the splitting of eight posts; each with three holes cut with an adze to take the rails, and the digging of eight holes; twenty one rails were split and sharpened at each end to fit into the holes in the posts. Working continually it was possible for two experienced men to erect twenty chains of fence in a month, which would earn them six pounds each, twice the wage of a shepherd.

To be myself answerable from the first day of washing till the last of shearing for all my expenses and those of every one of the men I will have engaged to shear —

To obey the orders of the Superintendent of the flocks or those of His Lordship —

His Lordship to be at liberty to admit more or less shearers or to send away those whose conduct or manner of shearing do not give Him full satisfaction, and Moreover He may admit to shear as many Aborigines as He may think proper —

Payment for the whole as above specified to be made to me after shearing and deducting all the expenses at the rate of four shilling and six pence (4/6.) per score and two (2) bottles of Colonial wine at the time of washing for every thousand sheep washed —

New Norcia 29 August 1863 —

Wm Boxhall

William Boxhal's last contract of employment with Bishop Salvado 29 August 1863. (Acc 2953A/5 Benedictine Archives New Norcia). Note the confident flourish in Boxhal's signature, which is so different from his earlier writing.

Two weeks later, on 17 May, they entered into another contract with Bishop Salvado and did:

> *agree to clear and burn all trees, making the ground ready for the plough at His Lordship's satisfaction on that part of the paddock beyond the vineyard at the rate of 47 shillings and 6 pence per acre to be ready before next summer.*

Whether Delaney and Boxhal were unable to work harmoniously or that the work they contracted was completed, the partnership did not last long. It was terminated by mutual agreement and recorded in the contract book on 20 October 1862.

On 19 April 1863 he commenced work for Bishop Salvado as a bullock driver and teamster at the a remuneration of 21 shillings a week, which was a very high wage. In the written contract he agreed that:

> *Rations and everything else I will want for myself I shall have to buy from the mission. I bound myself no (sic) to bring any thing on the team in my charge for any body without his Lordships per mission.*

Such work would have enabled him to take a team to Perth with a load of wool or other produce and return with goods for the Mission. As commercial cartage costs were high it is understandable that a teamster was not permitted to cart other peoples goods without permission or a charge at the going rate. As this contract commenced only three weeks before Boxhal was to marry it is feasable that he would have been able to take a team to Perth, be handsomely paid and return with his bride and permission to carry his own possessions.

The last recorded contract that Boxhal had with Bishop Salvado was on 29 August 1863, to:

> *wash and shear the sheep of New Norcia in a workman like manner.*

He would be responsible for his own expenses and could employ as many aborigines as he may think proper.

> *"Payment for the work as above expecified [sic] to be made to me after shearing and deducting all expenses at the rate of four shillings and six pence (4/6) per score.* In addition there was an interesting bonus of *two (2) bottles of Colonial wine at the time of making per every thousand sheep washed. (7)*

It is almost certainly the last contract (no others were discovered in the New Norcia records) because it was three months after he had married Mary Ann Kelly and would have commenced work as a farmer in his own right.

The difficulties that confronted William Boxhal, or any convict who had an ambition to become independent, purchase land and farm it were enormous. He had to overcome the stigma of having been a convicted criminal, irrespective of the nature of the offence; there was the disadvantage of little formal education and therefore having great difficulty in getting access to and understanding the intricacies and the consequences of applying for the purchase or lease of land. Over-riding all this was the daunting problem of having no capital whatsoever.

Boxhal entered the paid workforce with nothing except the clothes given him on arrival. The harshness of the climate and isolated bush living, which a young Englishman would not have experienced, and the arduous nature of the work demanded by the pastoralists, damaged many and even cost the lives of some convicts. He possessed a determination to succeed and although he lacked a basic education, he obviously had above average intelligence and understood what was required. He had exceptional physical strength and stamina. His achievments indicate that for the four years until he received his pardon, he must have applied himself with great diligence, lived frugally and squirreled away whatever cash he received.

The common wages paid to ticket-of-leave labourers was about eight shillings a week and keep. Boxhal's trade as a blacksmith may have enabled him to earn extra money fashioning implements and working as a farrier.

Because of the shortage of cash, many pastoralists often remunerated good shepherds with a portion of the increase in the flock that they husbanded. This would have only been suitable to those shepherds who had secured leases or freehold land or were prepared to squat on unclaimed land and had erected a fold in which to keep the sheep. Many shepherds did graze their stock without permission on unclaimed land and on land leased or owned by pastoralists.

A serious hazard that faced stock owners was the prevalence of poisonous plants, such as York Road Poison, Box, Prickly Poison and others. York Road Poison was so named in 1837 when stock being driven on the road from Perth to York died from having grazed on it. These plants were palatable and if eaten by sheep or cattle in its active growth stage, could kill an animal within hours.

The Victoria Plains correspondent to the *Inquirer,* in drawing attention to the plight of the farming community refers to one settler who, having suffered damage from the floods, which cost him three hundred pounds also had 130 sheep and eight cows die from eating poison vegetation. The previous year he lost 600 sheep. (8)

The shepherds became knowledgeable about which plants were poisonous and herded stock away from them. On their own small holdings the plants, which were recognisable by the yellow to red flowers, were laborously grubbed out and destroyed; if slashed, suckers would resprout.

There were, however, certain prerequisites that a man had to possess before he could acquire land and stock. A good horse, saddle and bridle were a priority to enable him to travel with any efficient use of time. The horse would also have to be suitable for pulling a cart and plough, which needed harness and some form of wagon. It was not uncommon for a shepherd to cull a colt from a pastoralist's mob of range-grazing horses, break it in at some isolated place and brand it. This was, however a dangerous practice because most pastoralists who bred horses for the Indian market knew their stock. If a former convict could not prove the purchase of his horse and was therefore accused of horse stealing he could have his ticket-of-leave or conditional pardon revoked, which meant a return to incarceration or work with the road gangs.

To grow any sort of crop he would have had to acquire or borrow a single-blade plough. There was a need to purchase basic implements, such as an axe, adze, cross-cut saw, sledge hammer and wedges, a shovel and sundry other tools. These were essential for him to construct the primitive, typical slab-built or mud-brick accommodation and erect fencing. It is probable that fencing for stock yards would have been "bush fences", made from thin Casuarina or River She-oak saplings that grew densely near the "Seven Mile Well". Pairs of six-foot-long poles were buried in pairs and spaced about three yards apart; other poles were placed in the gap until the desired height was reached and the tops of the uprights tied with wire or strips of greenhide.

The long thin casuarina saplings were also used in making furniture. It was tough and bent readily when green.

A rifle and ammunition were needed to shoot kangaroos and cockatoos for tucker and to protect the flock from marauding dingoes and wild dogs. Of great importance was a good sheep-dog to guard and herd the flock. It was common for all shepherds to own a dog of their own. The going rate for a good dog was about 2 pounds.

William Boxhal had worked with, and entered into a loose partnership with another former convict, Owen Lavin, who was the same age as Boxhal. He was transported for seven years for sheep stealing and came on the *Phoebe Dunbar* on 31 August 1853. He was given his ticket-of-leave in June the following year. (9) There are some stories passed on through the Kelly family to the effect that Lavin was often in trouble

49

with the law and a bad influence on Boxhal. There may be truth in this because he did not recieve a conditional pardon until ten years after his arrival. Lavin was illiterate and signed several New Norcia contracts to work as a shepherd with his mark.

It made sense for two former convicts, with little capital and the limiting convict stigma, to work together. They could develop a flock of sheep, which they would own jointly and would share the shearing, packing and carting the wool to earn a cash income. They would also share the work of building a shelter for themselves and fencing areas for the stock. Two men, working together, needed only one set of tools and could saw and split more timber slabs and posts than working on their own.

They squatted on or leased some land seven miles south of New Norcia on the road to Guildford where there was a good supply of water.

Regulations designed to encourage small farmers to purchase land were made in 1860 and the price of crown land was halved to ten shillings an acre. According to Rica Erickson, "only two small farmers had secured land [in Victoria Plains] by the end of the convict era in 1868. One was William Boxhal." (10) His first purchase of land was, however, done with Lavin.

The illiterate Lavin would have had a limited understanding of the procedures of the land acquisition systems and therefore prevailed on Martin Butler, who had purchased land and understood what was required to write to the Government on his behalf. Lavin had made some effort to purchase a freehold lot of forty acres, which was part of a lease near the "Seven Mile Well". But he wanted the title to be in his name and also Boxhal's name. The reason for the dual ownership was most probably because Boxhal had worked the land with Lavin and had built his house on it. It is also likely that it was Boxhal who had saved the cash needed to purchase the land. On 16 May 1865, Martin Butler wrote to the Government:

> *Sir,*
>
> *When you are for sending up the Free (sic) Simple of land I purchased I hope you will be so kind as to send it up in the name Owen Laven and William Boxhall.*
> *Please send too (sic) papers one each.*
> *Send your answer in care of Martin Butler V P*
>
> *for Owen Laven(11)*

It took a further year before the forty acre lot, Melbourne Location 77, on the road to Guildford was registered in their names for a fee of twenty pounds.(12) This was prime undulating land with good water.

They are referred to on the Title as farmers of Victoria Plains, which must have been a cause of pride and not a little rejoicing. At the time Lavin was working as a shepherd for the Benedictine Community. The New Norcia records of July 1865 show him as the shepherd for the sixth flock of 894 sheep. That year he had 17 die and lost 13. (13) He is recorded as a shepherd up until 1869, but is not recorded again until 1879, which is the last we hear of him. This does not mean that he did not work consistently for the Community. It could be that some of the books may have decayed over time.

Notes:
(1) E.J. Storman S.J., ed.&trans., *The Salvado Memoirs* University of Western Australia Press, Nedlands, 1978, p.84.
(2) George Russo, *Lord Abbot of the Wilderness,* Polding Press, Melbourne, 1980, p.67.
(3) New Norcia records, Acc., 2953A/5. He signed his name in these contracts as Boxhall.
(4) New Norcia records, Acc., 2953A/24.
(5) Rica Erickson and Gillian O'Mara, *Convicts in Western Australia 1850 - 1887 Dictionary of Western Australia Vol XI*, University of Western Australia Press, Nedlands, 1994.
(6) New Norcia records, Acc., 2953A/5.
(7) ibid.
(8) *Inquirer,* 18 September 1872.
(9) Rica Erickson and Gillian O'Mara, op. cit.
(10) Rica Erickson, *Victoria Plains,* Lamb Paterson Pty. Ltd., Osborne Park, 1971, p.35.
(11) J.S.Battye Library, SDUR/L3/346.
(12) Certificate of Title 1731.
(13) New Norcia records, Acc., 2953A/24.

Mary Ann

Ex-convicts, on the whole, had little prospect of marriage and faced a dreary future. Many of those employed in the Victoria Plains passed from the social scene without leaving a trace.

Rica Erickson *Victoria Plains* p31.

Soon after William Boxhal's arrival in the colony, dramatic events were developing in India that would have a profound effect on his life.

The Crimean war ended in 1856 with only nominal gains for Britain and France. Britain's forces stationed in India were weakened during the Crimean campaign and it was this and far reaching decisions of the British Government of India, which led to the rebellion of Indian troops in 1857. The first outbreak took place in May at Merut, where Indian regiments were in open revolt. Outbreaks occurred at Cawnpore and Lucknow.

Lucknow was defended, not only by an artillery battery, but by the tenth regiment, one of whose members was a Sergeant Thomas Kelly, who was born in County Wicklow, Ireland in 1819. The 1857 siege of Lucknow lasted from June to November with much loss of life. Kelly survived the bitter fighting and was commended for bravery.

Thomas Kelly and his wife Catherine, were said to have had 16 children, 13 of whom died.(1) With their three surviving children, a daughter, Mary Ann, and sons, Bernard and William, they retuned to Ireland. But soon after they were advised for health reasons to take their family to a warmer climate. Thomas Kelly re-enlisted in the Pensioner Guard and accepted an appointment to go to the Swan River Colony as a warder on the convict ship, *Lincelles*.

The *Lincelles* was one of larger convict ships, built at Moulmein in Burma in 1858. Under the command of Captain William Gardiner, it left Portland on 10 October, 1861, with 306 convicts, (three of whom died). There were 30 Pensioner guards, 17 women and 40 children. The ship experienced light and variable winds which caused a protracted passage of 115 days, stopping at Cape Town. The *Lincelles* made only one journey to Australia as a convict ship and was later used in the infamous India-Mauritius coolie trade in which it carried 400 coolies at a time.(2)

When they arrived at Fremantle on 29 January, 1862, the family was given a billet at the Mt Eliza Military Settlement (3)where they lived until Thomas Kelly purchased land on the South Perth Peninsula. On 20 May 1863, for £10, he was granted five acres, Perth Suburban Lot 95, overlooking the river. It was later subdivided into a large number very valuable residential lots fronting present day Mill Point Road, Swan Street and Leane Street.

We can only speculate about how William Boxhal met the Kelly family.

In 1862, two years after Boxhal received his conditional pardon he was working for Bishop Salvado and may have travelled to Perth with stock or for other assignment on behalf of the Benedictine Community, with whom he was held in high regard. This would have impressed the Kellys. A visit to Perth on his own behalf would have been costly. It would have been more than a day's ride on horseback, a journey, arduous for both horse and rider and one that would not have been done frequently. It would also not have been prudent to leave stock unattended for long periods. A flock of sheep could wander onto land with poison, be ravaged by dingoes or some acquired by other unscrupulous squatter shepherds.

He may have been introduced to the Kelly family by the former convict, Christopher Murray, who came out with the Kellys on the *Lincelles*. Murray was almost the same age as Thomas Kelly. He had been a farmer in the Falkland Islands and was the father of four, when he was convicted of manslaughter and transported for 14 years. He was given his ticket-of-leave four months after his arrival. As he was a Catholic and a more mature man than most of his fellow convicts it is reasonable to assume that Kelly may have befriended him on the journey out. He was a witness at Boxhal's wedding and must have been his friend.

However it may have happened, a romance did develop between the thirty-year-old William Boxhal and the sixteen-year-old Mary Ann Kelly and he proposed marriage. Despite the stigma of being a former convict, Boxhal had credentials sufficient to convince old Thomas Kelly that he would make a good husband for his daughter. He was a free man; Bishop Salvado had employed him and made representation on his behalf and he had been handed his certificate of freedom on

141.

Guilielmus
Boxhall,
4. Aprilis
1863.

Anno Domini Millesimo Octingentesimo Sexagesimo tertio, die quarta Mensis Aprilis, ego Bernardus Martinez Presbyter et Monachus Missionarius O. S. Benedicti, in Ecclesia SS Trinitatis Nova Nursia praedicti Ordinis baptizavi hominem Guilielmum Boxhall habentem triginta annos, filius Thomae Boxhall et Mathilda Pritchard ex Comitatu Kent in Anglia. Patrinus fuit Joseph Antonius Suarez filius Francisci Suarez et Maria Cabal ex Parochia S. Juliani de los Prados circa civitatem Ovetensem in Hispania, individuus hujus Missionis Benedictina in Australia Occidentali. N.B.

N.B. Baptizatus fuit
sub Conditione, Bernardus Martinez
post factam profes-
sionem fidei, et abju-
rationem protestantismi
cui pertinebat.

Certificate of Baptism of William Boxhal by Dom Bernard Martinez 4 April 1864

21 March 1863 (4); he was obviously fit and strong, had worked hard, saved money, acquired stock and the where-with-all to manage it and had built a small cottage on land south of New Norcia. With apologies to Henry Lawson he may have:

> listened to her father's yarns
> He did just what he oughter,
> And what he'd have to do to win,
> The tough old sergeant's daughter.

At about this time he had decided to become a Catholic. It could have been because of an association with the Benedictines and the Irish Catholic settlers in Victoria Plains, or he may have wanted to ingratiate himself with the Catholic Kelly family to seek approval to marry Mary Ann, or it may have been that Thomas Kelly had made it a condition if he wished to marry his daughter, or his decision was motivated by a personal faith conviction.

My own belief is that it was the latter. After years of association with the Benedictines, the strength and example of Bishop Salvado and the monks, especially Father Martinez would have influenced him. He was a man of such strong will and determination, that whatever decision he made, it would have been of his own making. Despite what ever Kelly demanded, he would have married Mary Ann, once he had decided to do so.

Whatever the reason, on 4 April 1863 in the church at New Norcia he was baptised by Father Bernard Martinez OSB. His Godfather was Joseph Suarez, a Bendictine Oblate or lay brother.(5) Father Martinez was a prominent priest at New Norcia and played an important part in the life of the Boxhal family, baptising and marrying most of their children and conducting the funerals of both William and Mary Ann.

The date for the wedding of William Boxhal and Mary Ann Kelly was set for 4 May 1863 in St John's Church, Victoria Avenue in Perth. The ceremony was performed by Father Martin Griver, who became Bishop of Perth on 1 October 1869. The best man was the former convict, Christopher Murray and the matron of honour was the wife of a Pensioner Guard, Mary Holloway.(6) The Holloways had come to the Colony on the *Emma Eugenia* in 1858. Three years later, John Holloway became the police constable in Toodyay.

It must have been a heart-wrenching moment for Catherine Kelly to see her only surviving daughter, who was so young, drive off with William Boxhal on a heavily loaded wagon, into the wilderness of Victoria Plains. Whatever she was told of the place, to her, the journey which would take two days or more, depending on the weather, would have been into a wild, dangerous, isolated and untamed country inhabited by black savages. The Kellys would have heard the stories of cannibalism practiced by the aborigines. Just five days before the wedding the *Inquirer* in the column "Local and Domestic Intelligence" carried a gruesome report of a Mr J.S. Davis who

> "came across a fire near which were portions of the bodies of two native women, evidently the remains of of some cannibal feast." (7)

This would have struck fear into the heart of a mother, whose only daughter was leaving to live where aborigines were numerous.

But to Mary Ann, who had married in love, it may have been more like how John O'Brien described:

> With trust in God and her good man
> She settled neath the spur;
> The old slab dwelling, spick and span,
> Was world enough for her. (8)

Yet she was so young and had barely experienced a normal childhood. She was born in India on 3 March, 1847 when her father was a private in the British army.

At the age of twelve she would have suffered the trauma of battle and seen the stark reality of death during the siege of Lucknow. To Dr Joseph Fayer, the civil surgeon in Lucknow it was a miracle anyone survived the siege that lasted for five months.

> By 22 July, the upper storey of the Residency's banquet hall, which had served as a hospital, was no longer tenable; sick and wounded huddled together on the ground floor. The children living on barley porridge seemed like wizened little old men ... Scurvey, now called "garrison disease", took its daily toll (9)

Alfred Lord Tennyson descibed graphically what she may have suffered, in the ballad *The Defence of Lucknow*:

> Frail were the works that defended
> the hold that we had with our lives-
> Women and and children among us, God help them,
> our children and wives ...

> Valour of delicate women who tended the hospital bed,
> Horror of women in travail among the dying and dead,
> Grief for our perishing children, and never a moment of grief.
> Toil and ineffable weariness, faltering hope of relief ...(10)

It appears that the Kelly children suffered from chest complaints because the advice given them in Ireland was that they should emigrate to a warmer climate or "they could lose the rest of their family."(11) Mary Ann was then fourteen; whatever education she had received - which would have enabled her to read and write - would have been further disrupted in the preparation for the journey to Australia.

Boxhal's wagon would have been heavily loaded and pulled by a team. He would have purchased some farming implements, furniture and such supplies of food, flour, tea, salt, sugar, and seed wheat that he hoped to plant before the winter rain set in.

As a blacksmith he would have scavenged any old iron that he could later fashion into things of use on the farm. It was the opportunity to purchase flat-iron for farriering, wire, nails and sawn planks to make furniture for their crude home. There would also have been some condiments and house-hold utensals of various kinds that a wife would see as important, but a man who had spent years roughing it in the bush, may not have thought necessary. With no grass after a long hot summer, they would have had to carry hay or chaff as feed for the team. Every item carried would have cost much less in Perth than New Norcia. They would also have had gifts from family and friends and Mary Ann's clothes and her few precious possessions.

The road to Guildford was well used and in good condition, which meant that they could travel at an easy pace. This journey was much different from the first time when he trudged wearily in a line of degraded convicts and ticket-of-leave men, seven years earlier. Now he was a proud free man with possessions and a new wife whom he loved. It is likely that they would have spent their first night in Guildford at an Inn and fed and rested the team for the long journey over the next two days.

From Guildford they would have taken the well-made road north, along the Swan Valley to Cruises Hill. This road had been built in 1845 to service the prime properties of some of the early prominent settlers. Boxhal's lumbering wagon laden high with a rough canvas cover for protection, would have contrasted with the elegant high-wheeled carriages, drawn by a pair of well bred horses that frequented the road. Once the Ellen Brook was crossed the journey would have been difficult if the first rains had come. The track through the flat clay land passed Bullsbrook and Wandena to the Chittering Valley, was not consolidated or drained and once wet was difficult to pass. Many a wagon became bogged. After a full day's travel they would most probably have camped near Chittering Lake. There the team was fed, watered and rested for

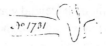

№ 1731

Victoria, BY THE GRACE OF GOD, OF THE UNITED KINGDOM OF GREAT BRITAIN AND IRELAND, QUEEN, DEFENDER OF T FAITH, &c., &c., &c. TO ALL to whom these Presents shall come, Greeting. KNOW YE that We, of Our especial Grace, certain knowledge and mere mot. have given and granted, and WE do by these Presents, for Us, our heirs and successors, in consideration of *Twenty Pounds* Sterling paid to the satisfaction of Our Governor of Our Colony Western Australia, GIVE AND GRANT unto *Owen Laven and William Boxal* of *Victoria Plains* in Our said Colony *Farmers* Dist ALL that Tract or Parcel of Land situate and being in the *Melbourne* in our said Colony, containing *Forty acres* more or less, AND marked and distinguis in the Maps and Books of the Survey Office of Our said Colony as *"Melbourne* Location N° *77"* AND BOUNDED on

West by a public road between Swan River and Morin Pool in Moore River On the South by a East line of twenty one chains fifty links from a part of the said road twenty chains North and about sixteen and a half chains East from a well dug in a water course near the Western side of road aforesaid said Well being about sixteen and a quarter of chains Northward from the seven mile mark on road aforesaid On the East by a North line of Twenty Chains and on the North by a West line to the aforesaid Road all bearings true.

Together with all Profits, Commodities, Hereditaments, and Appurtenances whatsoever thereunto belonging, or in anywise appertaining. TO HAVE ANI TO HOLD the said Tract or Parcel of Land, and all and singular the Premises hereby granted, with their Appurtenances, unto the said *Owen Laven and William Boxal their* heirs and assigns, for ever ; he or they yielding and paying for the same to Us, our heirs and successors, one pepper-corn of yearly rent on the Twenty-fifth day o March in each year, or so soon thereafter as the same shall be lawfully demanded. **PROVIDED, NEVERTHELESS,** that it shall at all times be lawful for U. our heirs and successors, or for any person or persons acting in that behalf by Our or their authority, to resume and enter upon possession of any part of the sai Lands which it may at any time by Us, our heirs or successors, be deemed necessary to resume for making roads, canals, bridges towing-paths, or other work of public utility or convenience, and such Lands so resumed to hold to Us, our heirs and successors, as of our or their former estate ; without making to the sai *Owen Laven and William Boxal their* heirs and assigns, any compensation in respect thereof ; so, nevertheless, that the Lands so to be resumed shall not exceed one-twentieth part in the whole of the Lands aforesaid, and that no such resumption be made of any Lands upon which any buildings may have been erected, or which may be in use as gardens, or otherwise, for the more convenient occupation of any such buildings ; and provided, also, that it shall be lawful at all times for Us, our heirs and successors, or for any person or persons acting in that behalf by our or their authority, to cut and take away any such indigenous timber, and to carry away, search and dig for any stone or other materials, which may be required for making or keeping in repair any roads, bridges, canals, towing-paths, or other works of public convenience and utility And we do hereby save and reserve to Us, Our heirs and successors, all mines of gold, silver, and other precious metals, in or under the said Land, with full liberty at all times to search and dig for, and carry away the same ; and for that purpose, to enter upon the said Lands or any part thereof.

IN WITNESS whereof We have caused our trusty and well-beloved *John Stephen Hampton Esquire* Governor and Commander-in-Chief of our said Colony, to affix to these Presents the Public Seal of our said Colony.

Sealed this *Eighth* day of *May* one thousand eight hundred and *sixty six* in the presence of the Executive Council.

L.S.

Signed A.S. 1731

Certificate of Title 1731 for Melbourne Location 77.

58

the long, steep, rugged climb through the hills to be negotiated slowly the next day. The Bindoon hills rose to a height of almost 1000 feet above sea level. They had to climb up a stony track that had earlier been hacked out by the Benedictines.

It is reasonable to presume that on the journey the new husband would have enthusiastically told his bride of his work for Bishop Salvado, his partnership with Owen Lavin; of the work they had done; of the stock they had acquired and the house he had built for her on the tillage lease that he intended to purchase.

Boxhal and Lavin would have built a rough humpy of wattle and daub, using the readily available bush timber, which they considered adequate for their needs and protection. But with the pending marriage, Boxhal would have left Lavin to occupy the hut on his own and built a more substantial home, suitable for his young bride. It would have been similiar to that which many that other poor early settlers had built.

I have located what remains of the house, which was on a rise on the eastern side of one of the creeks that flow into the Yarawindah Brook, at the southern end of Location 77, about one hundred metres from the road to Guildford.

Boxhal had dug a well into the brook for a water supply and used the clay that he removed to make sun dried bricks.

The house consisted of one room, fifteen feet by twelve feet and a verandah. There are signs that two small rooms were added at the north and south ends. It would have been made almost entirely from materials readily available and importantly without expending any cash. While some of the established settlers had substantial homes built of cemented stone -much of the work being done by ticket-of-leave men- and some of the buildings at New Norcia were made of burnt clay brick and sawn timbers, such materials would have been out of the financial reach of Boxhal.

Once laid on the stone foundation, the mud bricks were plastered. As Peter Cunningham recorded: "This plaster is composed of alluvial soil, mixed with a portion of cow dung to prevent it from cracking and with chopped grass to enable it to adhere, the coat being put on with a light spade ... On being quite dry white-washed with, plaster of paris or ashes and sour milk ... "(12)

A good fireplace and chimney were essential. These were made of field stone, which was plentiful, cemented with a slurry of clay soil and lime. Lime could be readily purchased in Perth for ten pence a bushell.(13) The roof would have been made of bush timber poles and either thatched from reeds that grew on the Moore River, about three miles away, or more likely from bundles of the long hair-like fronds of the casuarina trees that grew in abundance close by or made of bark stripped from trees.

Both methods were in common use and required no cash.

Window openings would have had wooden shutters. Framed glass was both scarce and expensive. The floors of most similiar homes were usually a mix of clay and green cowdung, rammed firm and rubbed to make a hard smooth surface.

> The old hand told me how to build a clean dirt floor;
> Beat it hard with spades and tread of feet,
> Then soak green cow dung and sweep again,
> Now sprinkle water, fire, and clean creek sand,
> And sometimes strew with cool green leaves;
> Sprinkle and sweep it twice a day
> Until, clean and sweet and hard,
> It gleams, black, polished like a board. (14)

After one hundred and thirty years of intense summer heat and and at times torrential rain and wind the mud brick walls have dissolved and been washed back into the creek from whence they came. All that remains today are the basalt rock footings and a collapsed fireplace.

The well that Boxhal dug in the creek-bed provided a good supply of fresh water, but the water would have been carried by bucket to the house and kept in a large wooden barrel that he may have been able to acquire from the Benedictines once it had been discarded for wine storage. The capture of rain-water from an unguttered roof would have been difficult.

The home that William Boxhal had built for Mary Ann' may not have been much different from the house in Henry Lawson's *The Drover's Wife*. As the years went by, Mary Ann too could have been left alone with four children and a snake in the house. Lawson writes:

> " It is near sunset, and a thunderstorm is coming. The children must be brought inside...she knows that the snake is there and may at any moment come up through a crack in the rough slab floor. She carries several armfuls of wood into the kitchen and then takes the children there. The kitchen has no floor - or, rather, an earthen one - called a "ground floor" in this part of the bush. There is a large roughly-made table in the centre of the place. She brings the children in and makes them get on this table ... She gives them some supper ... and snatches up some some pillows and bed clothes - expecting to see or lay a hand on the snake at any minute. She makes a bed on the kitchen table for the children and sits down beside to watch all night.

She has an eye on the corner, and a green sapling club laid in readiness on the dresser ...

Near midnight. The children are all asleep and she sits there still sewing and reading in turn. From time to time she glances round the floor and wall plate, and whenever she hears a noise she reaches for the stick. The thunderstorm comes on, and the wind rushing through the cracks in the slab wall threatens to blow out the candle...At every flash of lightning the cracks between the slabs gleam like polished silver. The thunder rolls, and the rain comes down in torrents." (15)

Boxhal's primary determination - apart from subsistence - was to establish himself as a land-owning farmer. This meant that he had to develop a flock of sheep, which would produce a cash income by the sale of some lambs and wool. The sheep were also a source of food and the fleece of slaughtered animals were used as bedding and like kangaroo and cattle hides were laid as floor coverings. His husbanding of the small flock was not much different from the shepherds of biblical times. Every sheep was known and they knew him and his dog. They had to be protected from the ravaging dingoes and kept from eating such foliage as York Road Poison; and there was always the possibility of theft. The cost of losing a sheep was equivalent to losing two weeks wages that a ticket-of-leave man received.

Boxhal would also have acquired some breeding cows, with the long-term objective of developing a commercial herd. There was a need to train young bullocks in yokes to pull a single blade plough and drag logs, and one of the many new tasks that Mary Ann had to learn was to persuade the house cow to enter a rough stall in the slab-built barn, tie down its hind leg and milk the animal for their own consumption.

In the first few months after settling in, William, typical of a new young husband not wishing to be separated from his wife, would have worked close to home. With the flush of new grass after first rains he did not have to move the sheep to far off pasture. There was also much work to be done at the homestead; the building of a barn for the animals, cutting post and rail fencing and sowing a small part of the cleared land with wheat, which later would hopefully provide grist for a coarse flour. The wheat would have been harvested by scythe and threshed on a stone and earthen floor of the barn. The grain gathered would have been taken to New Norcia or to the Clunes for milling.

It was later that Mary Ann, like other settler wives, would have suffered loneliness and fear caused by isolation from other human company, when her husband had to move a flock of sheep to more distant pasture after grass was eaten out, or had to travel to Perth or Toodyay to sell stock or conduct business.

By Christmas 1863, Mary Ann knew that she was pregnant with their first child. The news of this would have been conveyed to the Kelly family, who had built a wood and reed home on the South Perth Peninsula. Catherine Kelly, with deep maternal concern for her young daughter, would have insisted that she should return to Perth until her baby was born. William was conscious of their isolation and lack of support from other women, and before the first rains came, took her by cart on the two day journey back to Perth. Leaving her in the care of her parents he would have returned more quickly on horseback to tend to the ever pressing tasks on the farm.

Mary Ann's first child, a son, was born in the Kelly home in South Perth on 13 June, 1864. This was perhaps the proudest moment of William Boxhal's young life; he had withstood the degredation and the rigours of penal life and transportation, won his freedom, commenced a farm of his own - something he could not have done in England, married a young woman, whom he loved and had fathered his first born son, who would bear his name.

Two weeks later the child was taken to St John's Church in Victoria Avenue, where he was baptised and given the name William; Mary Ann's brother William was the Godfather.(16) The baptism was performed by Father Matthew Gibney, who was some five years younger than Boxhal and had only arrived in the Colony from Ireland on the *Tartar* on 12 December, 1863, six months after his ordination. Years later on 28 June 1880, while enroute by train to Sydney he received Australia wide fame when the outlaw, Ned Kelly, was wounded at the Glenrowan Hotel. Father Gibney left the train when it stopped at Glenrowen because he thought that there may have been wounded among the police and the outlaws. He entered the hotel where Kelly, who carried six bullets in his arms and legs, was thought likely to die. He heard Kelly's confession and annointed him. The train proceeded to Sydney without him.

The Catholic newspaper *The Record* in its editorial on 29 July, 1880 praised him for his courage:

> Before all this happened we knew that he was brave and devoted and charitable to an heroic degree. To us his generous characteristics did not require to be proved by any such extraordinary occurrence as took place at Glenrowen; they were already known on better and higher grounds; they were better known by the constant and

unflinching exercise of every priestly duty of charity, through all the years of a lengthened missionary career, of which we have been the witness.

Father Gibney later became Bishop of Perth, succeeding Bishop Griver on 23 January, 1887.

Although registration of births was compulsory, for some reason, most probably ignorance of procedures and probably Boxhal's anxiety to return to the farm, the child's birth was not registered.(17)

Notes:
(1) Letter from Mollie Gorman, granddaughter of Bernard Kelly, in the file of the author.
(2) Charles Bateson, *The Convict Ships 1787-1868*, A.H. and A.W. Reed, Sydney, 1974.
(3) Mollie Gorman op cit.
(4) Battye Library Occurrence Book Acc 1386 Volume 7 pp. 163 and 174.
(5) New Norcia Baptisimal Record Acc 2953/ 141.
(6) Certificate of Marriage, Registrar of Marriages Perth, 1993/1863.
(7) *Inquirer*, 29 April 1863, p.2.
(8) John O'Brien, "One by One" *Around the Boree Log*, Angus and Robertson, Sydney, 1950.
(9) Richard Collier, *The Indian Mutiny*, Collins, Fontana Books, London, 1966, p.205.
(10) Alfred Lord Tennyson, "The Defence of Lucknow." *Tennyson Poems and Plays*, Oxford University Press, London, 1973, p.482.
(11) Mollie Gorman op sit. This seems to indicate that Mary Ann may have had some bronchial complaint. The cause of her death at an early age was given as "supposed consumption".
(12) Derrick I. Stone and Donald S. Garden, quoted Peter Cunningham in *Squatters and Settlers* A.H.& A.W. REED PTY LTD., Sydney, 1978, pp.14-15.
(13) *Inquirer,* 30 December 1863.
(14) Derrick I. Stone and Donald S. Garden, quoted Lindsay Gordon in *Squatters and Settlers,* A.H.& A.W. REED PTY. LTD., Sydney, 1978, pp.44-45.
(15) Henry Lawson, "The Drover's Wife", *Henry Lawson's Best Stories*, Discovery Press Pty. Ltd., Penrith, 1968.
(16) Baptismal records, St Mary's Cathedral Perth. In later life he used the name William Thomas, but Thomas is not recorded in the Baptismal register.
(17) Registration of births was often left to the baptising clergyman, who because of overwork did not always attend to the registration.

8

Farmer and Grazier

William Boxhal was anxious to take his young family back to New Norcia, but there was the frustrating wait until the winter rain had ceased and the road became passable for his waggon. After the baptism of young William, he would most probably have returned alone to New Norcia on horseback to care for the new lambs and attend to the numerous other demanding tasks.

By the beginning of spring they would have made the long journey home. The route with the dark green and harsh grey trunks of the eucalypts was brightend by the splashes of yellow of the various acacias and the brilliant blue of the leschenaultia. The native grasses were lush, providing feed for their horses. The journey in spring was made more difficult than in summer because some six or more streams and the Brockman River had to be forded

Mary Ann, while attending to the needs of her young son, would have had to work to make the primitively furnished home comfortable and attend to the house vegetable garden and assist with other tasks. The Boxhals, like many other settlers, were essentially subsistence farmers who had to produce most of their own food.

There was a form of cooperative barter among the settlers who would share the killing of a sheep or a pig. Other than by drying or salting meat, it could not be kept for long periods. A pregnant sow was a prized possession because it could be fed on waste vegetables scrap or allowed to forage. Pumpkins were easy to grow and the English traditionally considered them as pig food. A sow could produce a litter of as many as ten piglets. The settlers also exchanged vegetables and dairy produce.

Boxhal saw it as a priority to produce adequate food for his family and ensure that his rough home would have provided secure protection from the elements. But he would have given greater priority to earning money to secure the land he farmed and acquiring the necessary tools and equipment to work it.

With his home close to the main route from the north to Guildford his trade as a blacksmith could earn him additional income. This meant making a slab-built shelter with a forge, made of the local basalt stone. Achieving the intense heat necessary in the forge required bellows, similar to what he and his father would have used in England. It consisted of two wooden slab sides joined with hide; each of the wooden sides had a leather flap inside over a hole that acted as valve to allow air to be sucked in with the first stroke and blown through the injecting piece of the bellows, which has been fashioned from pieces of iron pipe scavenged during his visits to Guildford and Perth. The purchase of a long-coveted and expensive anvil was more important than making or buying fine furniture for the home.

Stock being driven to the markets in Perth stopped at the "Seven Mile Well" adjacent to his property. The farrier work for wagoners and drovers, wagon repairs and wheelright work provided income, as would the sale of hay, surplus to his own needs.

The ardous task of clearing the land of the mature York Gum and White Gum was done by felling the trees with an axe and burning the stumps and waste boughs not suitable for fencing; a more efficient method, when the soil was damp, was to use a block and tackle and 100 feet of hemp rope, tied as high on the tree as possible. The roots of the tree were grubbed out and cut, and tension would have been kept on the rope tied to the base of a near tree with the block until the tree uprooted and fell. The sound trees were cut with a cross-cut saw into lengths suitable to be split for housing timber or fence posts. The green bark was stripped, heated over a fire and laid flat to be used for roof covering for house and barn.

Once the land was cleared and stumps burnt, the planting of a crop of wheat or oats would have been a long and physically demanding task. Ploughing was done with a horse or bullock drawn single blade, hand held plough. Seed was broadcast by hand in the ploughed furrows. The ripened crop was cut by scythe, raked with a wide wooden rake with wrought iron prongs, which Boxhal would have made and the stooks bound with a twine made from twisted stalk. Pitch forks were often made from a carefully selected hardwood sapling or bough of a tree that had two opposite branches from the main stem near the top.

The end with the boughs was heated over a fire, bent and tied to create a three pronged fork. While still hot, the prongs were curved and set between two logs or rocks and left for several months to dry. Once cured the end of each prong was sharpened. The harvest was

Once cured the end of each prong was sharpened. The harvest was threshed with a wooden flail on a stone and clay floor and the wheat gathered and stored in bags. The hay would have been stacked for feed for the stock. An implement of high priority but expensive, would have been a chaff-cutter to provide feed for the milking cows and horses.

Ten acres of crop was about as much as one man, working on his own could have managed. With good rains and without the use of fertilisers, ten acres of the good rich land Boxhal owned could produce as much as thirty bags of wheat, which would last a family for a year. Land was rarely cropped again the following year; had it been so the yield would have been poor. The settlers then lacked the knowledge - even if seed was available - that the sowing of legumes, such as clover, lupins and medic restored nitrogen to the soil. New land was cleared, burnt, ploughed and sown each year.

The wheat was taken to either Clune's mill or New Norcia to be ground into flour and some coarsely crushed to be used as porridge and a supplementary feed for the house cow and a bran mash for poultry. He later sold wheat to the Benedictines. The surviving New Norcia records show that in 1870 he sold 32 bushells of wheat to the Benedictine Community. In the same year his close neighbour, Tom Fitzgerald, sold 202 bushells. The only other record of a sale was in 1879 when Boxhal sold 53 bushells and Fitzgerald sold 201.(1)

Not being able to purchase fertilizer, animal manures were prized and cow pats were laboriously gathered, mainly by children. These were used in the house garden that produced crops of vegetables. The Irish influence in the area meant that potatoes, which were high in nutritional value, were planted in abundance. It was usual that when ploughing was completed, they would cut several furrows in the damper land near the "Seven Mile Well" and sow seed potatoes, kept from the previous year. In the summer months when mosquitoes were prevalent, dried cow dung was burned near the door of the house, the smoke being a deterent.

Being a blacksmith, gave Boxhal an advantage over other struggling cash-less pioneer settlers. He was able to fashion many implements and essential tools, such as wagon and harness parts, wedges, a maul and even the single-blade plough.

Four years after he and Lavin had purchased Melbourne Location 77, Boxhal purchased Melbourne Location 102, a ten acre lot on the northern boundary of Location 77, for the sum of seven pounds seventeen shillings. This lot also had a frontage to the road to Guildford.(2)

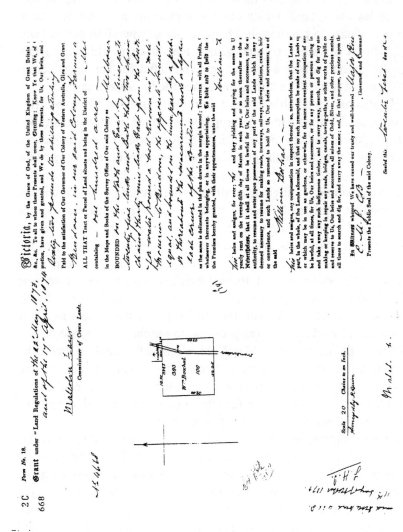

2C   Form No. 18.

668   Grant under "Land Regulations of the 21st May, 1872,
       and of the 19th April, 1874."

No. 4668

Walteton Lazar
Commissioner of Crown Lands.

Victoria, by the Grace of God, of the United Kingdom of Great Britain :
&c., &c. To all to whom these Presents shall come: **Greeting**: Know Ye that We, of
portion, have given and granted, and We do by these Present, for Us, Our heirs, and

Only ten pounds in consideration

Paid to the satisfaction of Our Governor of Our Colony of Western Australia, Give and Grant

ALL THAT Tract or Parcel of Land situate and being in the District of

containing — one hundred acres

in the Maps and Books of the Survey Office of Our said Colony as

BOUNDED

as the same is delineated in the plan drawn in the margin hereof; Together with all Profits,
whatsoever thereunto belonging, or in anywise appertaining. To have and to hold the
the Premises hereby granted, with their appurtenances, unto the said

William Bowhal

his heirs and assigns, for ever; He and they yielding and paying for the same to Us
yearly rent on the twenty-fifth day of March in each year, or so soon thereafter as the same
Nevertheless, that it shall at all times be lawful for Us, Our heirs and successors, or for any
authority, to resume and enter upon possession of any part of the said Lands which it may be
deemed necessary to resume for making roads, tramways, railways, railway stations, canals, bridges
or convenience, and such Lands so resumed to hold to Us, Our heirs and successors, as of
the said

his heirs and assigns, any compensation in respect thereof; so, nevertheless, that the Lands so
part, in the whole, of the Lands aforesaid, and that no such resumption be made of any Lands up
or which may be in use as gardens, or otherwise, for the more convenient occupation of any
be lawful, at all times, for Us, Our heirs and successors, or for any person or persons acting in
and take away any such indigenous timber, and to carry away, search, and dig for any stone
making or keeping in repair any roads, bridges, canals, towing-paths, or other works of public con
and reserve to Us, Our heirs and successors, all mines of Gold, Silver, and other precious metals
all times to search and dig for, and carry away the same; and, for that purpose, to enter upon the

In Witness whereof We have caused our trusty and well-beloved Major Gen
E. A. F. GB .   Governor and Commander
Presents the Public Seal of the said Colony,

Sealed this   Twenty first   day of

No. 4. 4.

Scale 20 Chains to an Inch.

363
Wm Bowhal
100

Certificate of Title 4668 for Melbourne Location 383.

When Boxhal was given a contract to go to Guildford and drive back a heavy dray and plant for the Victoria Plains Road Board, it gave him the opportunity to discuss the acquisition of freehold land with the Government Surveyor. By the early 1870s there had been only a small number of freehold lots granted to the Victoria Plains settlers. One of the main reasons was that most settlers were content to use the less secure leasehold land, which did not require the payment of a large amount of cash to purchase it. The purchase of a hundred acre lot was to later cost Boxhal, sixty two pounds ten shillings, which ironically was the amount of cash that he was convicted for having stolen in 1852, which resulted in him being transported to Australia.

He also had to be able to apply to the Government for a specified piece of land, which had to be properly described. Lots were not then being surveyed and offered for sale; if a settler wanted to secure freehold land, he had to describe the piece he sought and pay the ruling price for it.

Boxhal had an intelligent, intuitive understanding of the quality of the land that would make a productive farm. His shrewd assessment of its strategic position, the availability of water and the quality of the soil made him covet the land ajacent to the southern boundary of the Government watering reserve, known as "The Seven Mile Well". The soil was a heavy loam sand, formed over centuries by the weathering of the basalt rock. What he had to do was to formally apply to the Surveyor General and describe the specific position and measurements of a piece of land that he was prepared to purchase. (3) Once he had made the application he could stake his claim to the hundred acres, and if there was no other competing claiment, he was able to occupy and work the land with some sense of security before he received the title. It took a further eight years before the grant was made and he paid the sixty two pounds and ten shillings purchase price.

An indication of his success as a farmer and the extent to which his properties had been cleared, fenced and developed was that between 1868 and 1872 he was able to employ eleven ticket-of-leave men. (4)

Following his return with the Road Board dray, life seems to have run in a more orderly pattern for the Boxhal family. The size of his flock increased and he had harvested more wheat than his family could consume, selling the surplus to the New Norcia community.

It was more than four years before Mary Ann became pregnant again in 1874. Her pregnancy was sufficient reason for William to plan the building of a larger home on the proposed Melbourne Location 383. The site he chose was on the western side of the road to Guildford on

March 5 1884
seven miles on
Boomia

Mr John Forre[st]
Surveying general o[r]
commissioner of lan[d]
you will greatly
oblidge me if y[ou]
will be so good
to take up thes[e]
acres of waste lan[d]
for me
I have inclos[ed] th[e]
reant for it —
£3.2.6
Yreman yeu[r]
humble servent
William Boxh

William Boxhal's letter of 5 March 1884 to John Forrest applying for the lease of 3000 acres. This is the only hand-written letter discovered. It gives some indication of Boxhal's self taught rise above illiteracy.

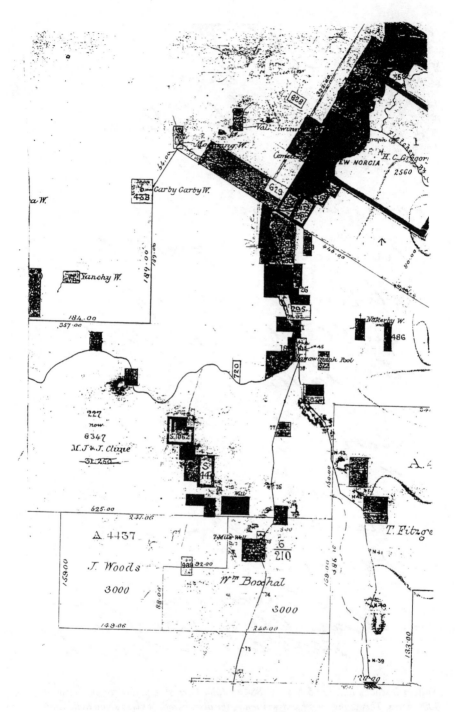

Map showing the extent of William Boxhal's land holdings.

the edge of a creek that fed the seven mile spring. The floor-space of the new home was more than three times larger than the small cottage that the five members of the family lived in.

It was forty feet by fifteen feet, with most probably a verandah at the front and rear. The construction was again sun-dried mud-brick laid on a stone foundation. Similiar to the first home, all that remains today are the basalt rock foundations, and a pile of rubble in the south west corner, which could have been a fireplace. The ravages of more than a hundred winters have dissolved and washed the bricks back to whence they came. The only sign of domesticity is a gnarled old almond tree, which has regrown from a large stump.

The method of construction would have again been to first dig a well into the creek bed during the dry season. The slurry of extracted clay was mixed in a wooden trough and shovelled into wooden box moulds; when set, left to dry on a flat area of ground. This arduous work had to be done during the summer. The magnitude of the task can be gauged by an estimate of the amount of clay required for the bricks, which was more than twenty tons. An additional ten tons was used in the compacted floor, which had to be thick enough to insulate the home from dampness and cold in winter.

The black stratified stone used in the foundations was readily available, but had to be gathered by hand, would have weighed about 25 tons. The stone was collected, most probably by his young sons, when ploughing was done. Such collections had the double effect of making the land more suitable for cropping.

It is likely that flattened bark was used for the roof. Although corrugated iron sheeting was available in the colony, it was expensive and the cost would have eaten into the cash he was saving to purchase the land.

When the house was completed it was furnished with shop-bought furniture, which not only made life easier for Mary Ann but more pleasing. For the first time she had a new bedstead and wash stand, a sofa, and a clock on the mantlepiece. The old rough-saw table was moved to the verandah as a work bench and replaced by a new polished table and the house was decorated with four paintings. (5) These are the items that we know were purchased, but there could also have been a stove with an oven and new crockery.

The decision to build a new and much larger home seems to indicate a change in Boxhal's priorities or that he had earned substantial cash and achieved the primary development of his farming objectives. It also indicates that he had a deep concern for the welfare of Mary Ann

The author at the site of the second Boxhal home on Location 383.
All that has survived are the stone foundations.

The remains of the Boxhal smithy on Location 77.

of _January_ 1884, to the _31st_ day

of _December_ 1884, in accordance with the Regulations for the

occupation of the same.

The position and boundaries are as shown ~~below~~:— _as per_

sketch attached.

boundaries:

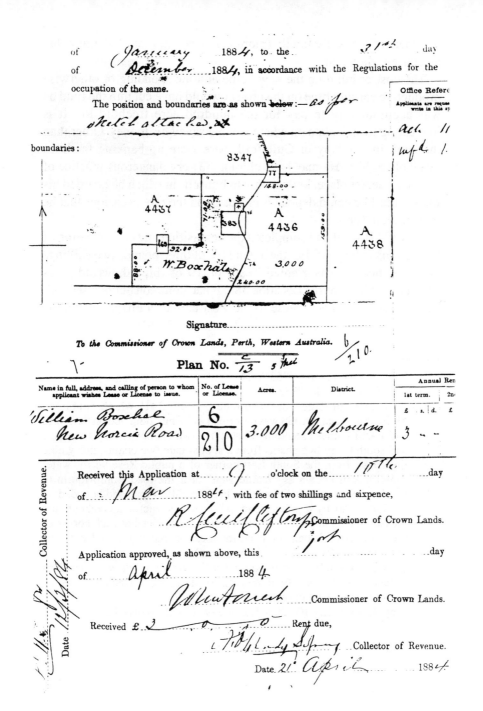

Signature

To the Commissioner of Crown Lands, Perth, Western Australia.

Plan No. $\frac{c}{13}$ 5 _sheet_

Name in full, address, and calling of person to whom applicant wishes Lease or License to issue.	No. of Lease or License.	Acres.	District.	Annual Ren	
				1st term.	2n
William Boxhal New Norcia Road	$\frac{6}{210}$	3.000	Melbourne	£ s. d. 3 - -	£

Received this Application at ___9___ o'clock on the ___10th___ day

of ___Mar___ 1884, with fee of two shillings and sixpence,

R. _Cecil Clifton_ Commissioner of Crown Lands.

Application approved, as shown above, this ___ day

of ___April___ 1884

John James Commissioner of Crown Lands.

Received £ _3_ _0_ _0_ Rent due,

Frd Ley Collector of Revenue.

Date _21 April_ 1884

_Extract of the Certificate of Lease 6/210 of the 3000 acres
leased by Boxhal on 10 March 1884_

members of the Kelly family (more than a century later) alleging that he abused Mary Ann.

The cost of building the new home and the spending of otherwise productive earning time on the project would have cut into the fund he was accumulating to pay for the hundred acre freehold lot. It is interesting to speculate on where Boxhal saved his money. Other than the bank in Toodyay or Guildford there were no banking facilities available to him. He may have chosen the very dangerous practice of digging a secret place, known only to himself, in which he hoarded his money until he could deposit it in a bank on the rare occasions that he visited Guildford.

By 1884 Boxhal had completed the acquisition and consolidation of his farming enterprise. For the annual fee of three pounds two shillings and sixpence he was granted Lease 6/210 of three thousand acres surrounding Melbourne Location 383. It had common boundaries with John Wood's 3000 acre lease to the west and Tom Fitzgerald's 6000 acre lease to the east.(6)

Notes:
(1) New Norcia records, 2953 A/24.
(2) Certificate of Title, 2832.
(3) Certificate of Title 4668 (Volume 5 Folio 341) which contained Melbourne Location 383 was described as being "Bounded on the North and East by lines extending West thirty two chains, twenty five links and south thirty two chains from a spot situate two chains, thirty nine links East from the South East corner of a public Reserve for water round a well known as "7 mile well" near the road from Mourin to Bindoon, the opposite boundaries being parallel equal and bounded on the inner part by a public road. All bearings true or thereabouts the measurements more or less and squared post placed at each corner of the Location." (When surveyed the location was not bounded by the public road. The road passed through it.)
(4) Rica Erickson,*The Bicentennial Dictionary of Western Australians Volumes 1-4,* University of Western Australia Press, Nedlands,1988.
(5) These items are mentioned in his will.
(6) Map, Cons 4922 / 10 000863, Lease 6/210 C.S. Battye Library.

9

St Joseph's School

By 1871, the Boxhals and their three children were part of a community of Irish-Catholic settlers. Many of their descendents were later woven into a colourful and complex genealogical tapestry by marriage. Mary Ann's parents and her brothers were well established south of Boxhal's property. Thomas and Margaret Fitzgerald owned Melbourne Locations 502 and 150 on the Old Victoria Plains Road less than a mile to the east of the Boxhal's home. The Fitzgerald's eventually had ten children, one of whom, Ellen, married young William Boxhal in 1884.

Near the junction of the Old Victoria Plains Road and Guildford Road, close to Yarawindah Pool, were the properties of the Clune brothers, Thomas Leahy and his brother in law James Maher. The youngest of the Boxhal girls, Julia Ann, later married James Maher's son, Richard. A short distance to the west of Boxhal's property, John Woods had Melbourne Locations 217 and 196. There were other families, such as Lanigan, Joyce, Sheridan, Halligan, Hunt and Thompson, but the most prominent and successful of this localised community were the Butler and Clune families.

When the Victoria Plains Road Board was formed in 1871 and at the first election, conducted by the Toodyay resident magistrate at the New Norcia police station, Martin Butler was elected secretary, his father-in-law, Jeremiah Clune, was a Board member and Matthew Clune, auditor. The other Board members were Donald Macpherson (chairman), Bishop Salvado, James Clinch, W Padbury and James Drummond.(1)

The number of children of the Victoria Plains settlers had increased and none were recieving any formal education. The more fortunate were given home teaching which was little more than the learning of numbers, some reading and writing. Most of the early settlers, many of whom were only semi-literate, had little time to devote to the education of their children. The growing number of unschooled children generated a demand for a local school. An unnamed Victoria Plains correspondent to the *Inquirer* in May, 1872, reported that:

> The Roman Catholics have been stirring themselves with a view to provide for the intellectual wants of the children, who have been hitherto growing up in ignorance. The result of their exertions appears already in the building of a school and dwelling house for the teacher, which are both in the course of erection on a spot which has been considered as the most central. (2)

This "spot" was near the Yarrwindha Pool close to the junction of The Old Plains Road and the road to Guildford on land donated by the Clune family. The move to establish the school was initiated by Father Raphael Martelli, an Italian secular priest, who had spent some time with the Benedictines at New Norcia.

The architect and supervisor of the building operation was the versatile priest and friend of the Boxhal family, Dom Bernard Martinez of the Benedictine community, who had already had a profound influence on the Boxhal family. The settlers were fortunate to have such a person in charge of the work because the incessant rain during the winter of 1872 caused devastating flooding of the Moore River and inundated the partly-finished school building. Rica Erickson gives Father Martinez the credit for its survival because he "had directed that the walls should be doubly thick, and of burnt bricks, for the customary mud bricks would have been washed away in the onslaught of waters."(3)

The efforts of the Catholics of Victoria Plains to establish a school was not solely motivated by the needs of their children. The more informed among them, like Martin Butler were aware that delegations on behalf of Bishop Griver and separately by Bishop Salvado to Governor Weld had been made seeking assistance to the growing number of Catholic schools that had been established in the colony. The Victoria Plains Catholics were a microcosm of the wider Catholic community, which throughout Australia had campaigned without success for assistance to Catholic schools.

The efforts of the Catholics in Western Australia, did however result in a measure of assistance from the Government, albeit for only a period of 24 years. After much acrimonious debate and bitter sectarianism the *Elementary Education Act, 1871* was passed, which provided Catholic schools with yearly per capita grants of one pound, seven shillings and six pence per pupil, half the amount paid to Government schools.

The Victoria Plains correspondent to the *Inquirer* vehemently expressed the feelings of the Catholics to the passing of the Act:

> ...under the Elementary Education Act it is more than doubtful whether [we] will be able to support a schoolmaster, the capitation grant for assisted schools being so small. Will the future Legislature correct the faults committed by the past one in placing the ... schooling of a position so inferior to Government schools? ... Is not this a flagrant injustice?...The debate which took place on this point in the Legislative Assembley is fresh in the public memory will not, perhaps, be overlooked on the occasion of the forthcoming elections.(4)

It was so much futile huffing and puffing because the Catholics were politically impotent and unable to have much effect on the decisions of the Parliament. There were no Catholics in Legislative Council at the time and many, like William Boxhal, were not even registered to vote. So powerless were they that by 1895, the assistance that Catholic schools received from the Government was abolished by the passing on 1 October 1895 of the *Assisted Schools Abolition Act.*

William Boxhal and all other Catholic settlers, who lived in the near vicinity, participated in the building of the school and a small cottage for a teacher. The costs were raised by donations and various fund raising activities of the Catholic community. The school was originally known as St Joseph's School, but later the name was changed to the Victoria Plains School. It was opened with a gala celebration in October 1872. Father Martinez blessed the building; hymns were sung and tea was served in the classroom which was not big enough to hold the large crowd.

Martin Butler, who was then 48 and had been in the Colony for 26 years, resigned his position on the Victoria Plains Roads Board and became the first teacher, a position he held until 1878 when he resigned because of failing eyesight. In 1879 his daughter, Mary Butler, became the school mistress and remained until she married in 1884. She was succeeded by Miss Elizabeth McKnight.

Although the 1871 Act made it compulsory for children to the age of fourteen to attend school, many of the children, like Thomas Boxhal (5) avoided regular, if any, attendance at the school in preference to farm work and hunting kangaroos and cockatoos or catching gilgies in the Moore River. Kangaroo skins could be sold for as much as five shillings (6) and the white cockatoos, which were often in plague proportion and destructive to crops, could be sold as pets to people in Perth and Fremantle.

St Joseph's School has survived the ravages of time.
Photographed by the author in 1999

The struggle to maintain the school came to an end, because of falling numbers and the inability of the people to finance the cash shortfall. The final blow came with the passing of the *Assisted Schools Abolition Act..* Martin Butler died in April, 1895, six months before the bitter sectarian debate and the passing of the Act.

The old school building still stands today in a dilapidated state, but the unbaked bricks used for small cottage, built for the teacher, have suffered the ravages of a hundred years and dissolved back into the ground. All that remain are the stone foundations.

When the Victoria Plains Roads Board was formed in February, 1871, the first purchase of road making-equipment was a heavy horse drawn dray, which had to be driven from Guildford. The contract to bring the dray to New Norcia was awarded toWilliam Boxhal for a fee of one pound ten shillings. (6) The fee was only equivalent to about a week's pay that he had earned as a shepherd, but what was of great value was the opportunity to be paid to travel to Guildford and purchase things that were required for the farm and the home that could not be purchased in New Norcia. The cartage cost for goods to New Norcia was then twenty pounds a ton.

Such a contract was also a tribute to Boxhal's horsemanship because a heavy dray, most probably loaded with other purchases made by the Road Board, would require a team of at least six horses to pull it up the steep hills from Chittering. This demanded considerable skill and expertise. It was a difficult task for one man to harness and contol unfamiliar or ructious, badly trained horses. At every resting place on the journey, the horses would have been uncoupled to drink and be fed and then be reharnessed.

Like most settlers' children, young William, who was then seven years old, would have learned to ride a horse almost as soon as he could walk. Probably he would have been invited to accompany his father; an exciting adventure for a boy to sleep out for several nights and see a large town for the first time. It was a learning experience for the boy and he would have been company for his father on the long journey.

The decision to purchase the dray was made in February, 1871. It was a matter of priority that it be brought up in autumn before the first rains, which would turn the flat country between Upper Swan and Bullsbrook into a quagmire. If it was not done in the dry season, the plant would have to stay in Guildford until late spring or early summer. At that time of the year the father and son could sleep out without needing protection from rain. It also meant that some of the watering holes for the horses on the road could be dry. The road had been much used by pastoralists, bullock teams and stock drives since the young Boxhal family first travelled it seven years earlier, but it was still not much more than a worn track. Parts of it had been stabilised and some of the water courses that crossed it had been bridged or forded.

Mary Ann, who would remain at home with five-year-old Matilda and Thomas, who was not yet two, prepared her two men for the journey on horse-back. She would have made coarse grain biscuits, and provided them with some salted meat, fresh fruit, potatoes, flour and dried sultanas for damper. They would have carried a waterbag and billy for tea. The young boy would have proudly ridden off with a blanket roll tied on the back of his saddle with strips of green hide.

Their first night would have been spent at Lake Chittering. Boxhal prepared the evening meal and made a camp fire on a piece of flat rock, with a billy of water for tea suspended above it on a forked stick. Whole potatoes were placed in the fire and when most of the wood had burnt to charcoal, the ashes were scraped away and the damper, a mix of flour and water with a little salt and the sultanas for flavouring, was kneaded into a round slightly flattened cake and placed on the heated rock. The glowing embers were heaped back over it until when William inserted a knife, which showed that there was no sign of uncooked dough. When cooked it was removed from the fire and thoroughly dusted off, broken in pieces and enjoyed with the baked potatoes and a mug of tea. It was a feast to delight a seven-year-old boy.

It was an easier ride to Guildford the next day. They would have trotted more quickly, stopping at watering places to refresh the horses. On some of the flat country they could break into a canter. Early arrival in Guildford was important for Boxhal. Not only did he have to complete the arrangements to take delivery of the dray and the team of horses, but he was anxious to use the time to purchase supplies of essential goods that were cheaper in Guildford, such as several pieces of furniture and more important to Boxhal, farming implements and discarded iron that could be used in the forge. He would have used the time to discuss the purchase of land at the office of the Government Surveyor.

Notes:

(1) Rica Erickson, *The Victoria Plains,* Lamb Paterson Pty. Ltd., Osborne Park, 1971, P.38.

(2) *Inquirer,* 1 March 1871.

(3) Rica Erickson, op. sit., p.39.

(4) *Inquirer,* 25 May 1872.

(5) Thomas was illiterate. As the informant on the death certificate of his father in January 1893 he makes his mark X.

(6) Rica Erickson, op. sit., p.39.

10

Family

Almost two years after young William was born, Mary Ann gave birth to their first daughter, Matilda Catherine on 15 March 1866. (1) We can assume that the child was born in the small Boxhal home and that May Ann's mother, Catherine Kelly, was there to assist her daughter. The Kellys had sold their South Perth property to Thomas Bishop on 19 October, 1865, for thirty two pounds (2) and had leased land near the road to Guildford, south of the Boxhal property. It is also likely that a close neighbour, Margaret Thompson, would have been there, assisting as a midwife.

Margaret Thompson was an interesting person in the New Norcia community and other far flung areas. She was formerly Margaret Murphy, who arrived in the colony at the age of 20 years and married the 38-year-old Robert Thompson on 18 November, 1855. Thompson was a former convict, who came on the *Sea Park* in March, 1853. Margaret Thompson's sister, Catherine, also married a former convict, William Hunt, who farmed in partnership with Thompson; they later purchased the farm and homestead known as Choral, east of New Norcia from Bishop Salvado. But Margaret's claim to fame was that although she had eleven children of her own in the span of 19 years, she acted as a district midwife, travelling as far as Three Springs.

The sixth child in the Thompson family, Alice Margaret, who was born in 1864, was to later marry the fourth of the Boxhals' children, Thomas.

Matilda was a sickly infant and considered by those at the birth was likely to die. The following day she was taken on the seven mile journey to the church of The Most Holy Trinity in New Norcia to be baptised by Father Martinez. Thomas Fitzgerald was the Godfather.(3)

Mary Ann was like many of the pioneer women settlers, who saw the birth of children as a natural function and on average gave birth to a child almost every two years.

Dom Bernard Martinez OSB. He played a significant role in the life of William Boxhal, baptizing him in 1863 and conducting his funeral in 1892. During that time he baptized most of the Boxhal children, married some and buried Mary Ann Boxhal.

Within two years of the birth of Matilda, Mary Ann had another daughter, Joanne, on 31 January 1868. (3) She too was in poor health and was taken to New Norcia to be treated by the Benedictine priest, Emiliano Coll, who had medical knowledge. Father Coll baptised her and the Benedictine brother, Joseph Suarez, who stood as Godfather to William when he became a Catholic was also Godfather to Joanne. Margaret Maher, who lived a mile north of Boxhals near the junction of the Victoria Plains Road was the Godmother.(4) Little could be done for the child; with a devastating impact on Mary Ann, she died four months later on 18 March and was buried at New Norcia by Father Martinez.

Infant mortality was the ever-present fear of settler women. It was common and was usually caused by influenza, diphtheria, measles, dysentery and water-borne infections. Isolated from any established town, they did not have the help of professional medical advice or effective medication.

Their second son Thomas was born on 12 September 1869 and was baptised at New Norcia on 2 November by Father Martinez. This time Margaret Branson, the wife of a former convict, William Branson was the Godmother.(5) Branson was among the first batch of convicts who came to Western Australia on the *Scindian* in June, 1850. He worked as a carter in the New Norcia area and later was employed by Boxhal.

There can be no doubt that William Boxhal worked long hours performing heavy manual labour - he would not have succeeded had he not done so - and most probably expected the same kind of hard work, understanding of what was required and dedication from those close to him. We should spare a long sympathetic thought for Mary Ann. When her third child, Joanne was born she was only 20 and did not enjoy good health, having almost certainly contracted tuberculosis in India; yet as a subsistance farmer's wife, she was expected to care for three young children; conserve the food resources, which meant such things as learning - without training and limited guidance - to make butter and possibly cheese, bake bread and preserve meat without any form of cooling or anything remotely like what we know in the twentieth century as refrigeration. She had to tend to the house vegetable garden, the poultry and the milch cow; she had to carry water from the well by bucket and do all the normal domestic chores of cooking meals, washing and making garments.

In the early days of the struggle to establish the farm there was little cultural development in the home; no music and barely anything that could be called literature. There may have been a Bible and a Sunday

Missal, but if there were other books or outdated newspapers, and they had the desire to read, there was little time or energy to do so. At the end of a long day of hard work, the want would have been to eat and sleep. In any case the smelly fat lamp or candles would not have given adequate light. This gradually changed as they became more soundly established and when children attended school.

The settler women visted each other, which provided companionship, support and a form of learning. Travelling the seven-mile journey to church on Sundays was always an outing, dressed in what they considered to be their "Sunday best", and an opportunity for socialising. Indeed the weekly attendance at Mass at the Church of The Most Holy Trinity at New Norcia provided the opportunity to meet people of a like mind and share problems; and the preaching, the reciting of prayers and the singing of hymns were an important form of cultural development.

After the birth of Thomas in 1869, life became more ordered and possibly a little more prosperous. Thomas was almost five years old when Mary Ann became pregnant again. During the heat of December, 1874, Mary Ann gave birth to a daughter, who was baptised Catherine in the church at New Norcia by Father Martinez five days before Chrismas.(6) Mary Ann's brother Bernard was the Godfather and the eldest of the Thompson children, Ellen was the Godmother. Poor Catherine is one of the unfortunate children of the Boxhal family; among other problems that she faced later, it seems that she contracted the tuberculosis bacillus from her mother.

Two years after the birth of Catherine, on 16 October 1876, when they were settled in their new home that had been built on the 100 acre Location 383, Mary Ann gave birth to her namesake. The child was baptised by Father Martinez on 12 November and given the names Mary Ann. (7) On this occasion James Hunt and his sister Mary were the Godparents.

The late 1870s was a time of increasing prosperity for the Boxhal's. The size of the flock of sheep and the number of cattle had increased providing a ready cash income which, not only enabled them to pay the purchase price of the hundred-acre lot, but also meant the purchase of some better furniture for the house and the occasional "Sunday best" dress for Mary Anne. Boxhal was even able to employ several ticket-of-leave men to work on the property. This reduced his workload, but also freed him to earn cash as a blacksmith and do more lucrative occasional work for the Victoria Plains Road Board.

Despite the harshness and the dramatic changes in his early life, and the dehumanising imprisonment and transportation, Boxhal does not seem to have forgotten his family roots. Two of his children, Thomas and Matilda, could have been named after his mother and father; although it is just as reasonable to assume that Thomas was named after Mary Ann's father, Thomas Kelly. Two of his daughters Julia and Mary Ann also had the same names as Boxhal's sisters. Sadly there is no evidence that he wrote to his family once he was settled in Australia. That there is no evidence does not mean that he did not communicate with other members of his family.

Almost two and a half years after the birth of Mary Ann and again in the heat of summer Julia was born on 21 December 1878; she - like most of the Boxhals - was baptised by Father Martinez and as for Catherine, Bernard Kelly and Ellen Thompson were the God parents.(8)

Mary Ann's health was not good, but despite her decline she was to have two more daughters. Elizabeth was born in the early summer of 1881 and was baptised by Father Martinez on 11 December, 1881. On this occasion Richard Lanigan and Anna Fitzgerald were the Godparents.(9)

In the spring of 1884 the Boxhals and their closest neighbours, the Fitzgerald family prepared for the great celebration of the joining of the families. Young William, who was then 20, had proposed marriage to Ellen Fitzgerald. With William's friend Richard Lanigan as the best man and Ellen's sister, Mary the bridesmaid, they were married in the Church of the Most Holy Trinity at New Norcia on the 16 September 1884 after the publication of Banns. (10)

Marriages were an occasion in the community for celebration and the first Boxhal nuptial would have been no exception. There would have been much rejoicing and the colonial wine would have "flowed like buttermilk". Following the Nuptial Mass and the marriage ceremony, which was performed by the long-time friend and mentor of the family, Father Martinez, the guests repaired to Clunes paddock and St Joseph's school house. The festivities were a communal affair with the guests contributing to the food. The school chairs were pushed back against the walls and the desks were assembled to carry the food, in the centre of the hard mud floor, which had been polished for the dancing that followed. While the women prepared the food inside the school house and talked enthusiastically about the many things common to farming wives the men gathered in groups, smoked and talked of cattle, sheep and the season, which in September, with lush green crops

Yamarah, *the first home of the Fitzgerald family.*
(Photograph 1980s courtesy of Patricia Cole.)

and pasture was promising. The children played near the swollen Moore River; some returning muddied and in trouble with their elders.

The bride and groom and their attendants arrived, sitting stiffly in a scrubbed clean buggy. Dancing followed the feast and the clumsily delivered speeches, liberally toasted. The music was provided on the school piano by one of the musically talented Fitzgerald family and the fiddle, most likely played by old Thomas Kelly.

In a way Boxhal was disappointed and a little depressed at losing his son, who had been his most effective worker on the farm. There was no room in the already crowded Boxhal farmhouse for the newly-married couple and the Fitzgeralds who had built a new home, had given their first farm house on Yamarah to the newlyweds. William leaving the Boxhal home was more disappointing because it coincided with the completion of negotiations to secure the 3000 acre lease.

Perhaps because of her poor health and declining fertility, it was almost five years before Mary Ann became pregnant again. Her last child, whom they named after their new daughter in law, Ellen (The New Norcia baptism records, which are written in latin use the name

Ellen Mary Boxhal (nee Fitzgerald) about 1895
Photograph courtesy Patricia Cole

Hellena) was born on 22 August 1886 and bapitised by Father Martinez on 2 September, 1886.(11) Only Mary Maher stood as a Godmother.

In the new year, William Boxhal and his family, were overwhelmed with tragedy. Ellen, who was a sick baby from birth, died and was buried by Father Martinez on new years day 1887. Like all mothers who lose a child, no matter how forewarned, Mary Ann was distraught with grief at the death of her daughter. She was confined to bed and was attended by neighbours and family.

Father Emmillio Coll, who was trusted for his medical knowledge, was called to treat her and diagnosed her symptoms as being what was then known as consumption.(12)

Nothing could be done to alleviate her fever and the coughing up of blood. One month after the death of her daughter, Mary Ann died on 3 February at the age of 40.

Her children were hysterical at the news that their mother had died, but the one who was effected most was William Boxhal; he had lost his wife of twenty four years, whom he may have taken for granted, but she had been his loyal helper in creating the farm, his lover and the mother of his children. She was one flesh with him and now she was gone. The agony was greater than whatever he had suffered as a convict.

Notes:
(1)   New Norcia baptisimal records, 2953A/28.
(2)   Conveyance Book no 1908, p. 308.
(3)   New Norcia baptismal records, 2953A/28.
(4)   ibid.
(5)   ibid.
(6)   ibid.
(7)   ibid.
(8)   ibid.
(9)   ibid.
(10) Certificate of Marriage, Registrar of Marriages Perth, 5855/1884.
(11) New Norcia baptismal records, 2953A/28.
(12) The Death Certificate, 122/1887, records the cause of death as supposed consumption.

11

Finale

The death of Mary Ann had a devastating effect on William Boxhal. Despite her failing health and persistant cough it was something he had not anticipated. He did not think that she would die. She had been his soul-mate, whom he had loved. He had taken her for granted and had relied on her to do so much; to do his bidding; to console him when he needed to be consoled; to be mother of and for his children. Now his wife for almost a quarter of a century was gone forever.

At 55, in the time in which he lived and after a life of grinding hard work, he was an old man. With Mary Ann's death, he let go the reins for the first time in his life; he felt old and worn-out and consumed with grief.

His son William was married and Matilda at 21 was a mature woman who could care for herself. Thomas was a young man of 16 years, who could also care for himself. But he had four young daughters, Catherine 13, Mary Ann 11, Julia 8 and Elizabeth 6, whom he had to care for. It was a task he had not performed and one he felt incapable of performing.

Father Martinez came to console him and arrange for Mary Ann's funeral Mass in the Church of the Most Holy Trinity. As usual the church was crowded with family and friends. The sacramental life of baptisms, marriages and funerals was always shared by those in this close community. It would have been usual for a wake to be held, but a wake could not alleviate Boxhal's grief

Headstones were expensive and had to be made by stone-masons in Guildford or Perth, but Boxhal had one erected, which simply said:

" Sacred to the memory of Mary Ann Boxhal who died on the 3rd February 1887 aged 40 years".

The spelling of the name was that used on her wedding certificate and also on her death certificate.

The farm that he had worked so hard to create and successfully develop into one of the prized properties in the district now meant little. He could look out over rolling pasture and stock grazing, but wth Mary Ann's passing his ambitions had dissolved and with it the indomitable spirit and determination, which had sustained him during his incarceration and enabled him, against great odds, to become a successful farmer. The occasional indicators of sickness and discomfort had been ignored and to some extent overcome by sheer willpower.

The sting of death was however, salved a little by the birth of Boxhal's first grandchild. It was another joyful milestone in the harsh struggle of his life. William and Ellen Boxhal's first child was born at the Yamarah farm-house and baptised by Father Martinez, who had become an institution in the Boxhal family, on the 15 July 1888. She was named Mary Ann after her recently deceased grandmother. (1)

At about this time he contemplated leaving the farm and moving to live in Guildford. He was concerned for the welfare and the education of his two youngest daughters, Julia and Elizabeth. His health had deteriorated and he could receive better treatment from a doctor in the town.

He was annoyed and dismayed by the decision of Matilda, who at 23 years of age, intended to leave the farm to marry Henry Playford. Playford was the son of Henry Playford, who was one of the first convicts to arrive in the colony on the third convict ship, the *Mermaid* on 7 May 1851. Boxhal's objection to the marriage was not because Playford was the son of a convict,(2) but because he was not a Catholic. Poor Matilda was said to have been banished and she married Playford in Perth on 24 April 1889. She and Playford were however, married in the Catholic Cathedral. When she died on 15 September 1930, she was buried in the Roman Catholic section at Karrakatta Cemetery.

The deep prejudice Boxhal held meant that he may not have seen his first born grandson, George Henry Playford, who was born in Upper Swan on 12 February 1890.(3)

Soon after, on 3 April 1890, Thomas Boxhal and Alice Margaret Thompson were married by Father Martinez at New Norcia. (4) Alice was the daughter of a former convict, Robert Thompson.

A neighbour, John Woods, who had commenced farming at about the same time as Boxhal, had some freehold land to the west and a three thousand acre lease with a common boundary with Boxhal's lease. Woods desired Location 383, adjacent to the "Seven Mile Well", because of its frontage to the main road, the quality of the soil and the water.

A Memorial to be registered of an Indenture of Conveyance duly stamped with a duty of £1. 7. 6 made the 10th day of February 1892 Between William Bothal of Bindoon in the Colony of Western Australia Farmer & Grazier of the one part and John Woods of Victoria plains in the said Colony Farmer of the other part. thereby after reciting that the said William Bothal is seized of an estate in fee simple in possession as joint tenant with own Lavern late of Victoria plains aforesaid Farmer in the said lands and hereditaments mentioned and described in the first Schedule thereto and hereto And reciting that the said own Lavern died at   on or about the   day of   18   And reciting that the said William Bothal is also seized of an estate in fee simple in possession in the lands and hereditaments mentioned and described in the second Schedule thereto and hereto And reciting that the said William Bothal had agreed with the said John Woods for the absolute sale to him of the said lands & hereditaments and the inheritance thereof in fee simp. in possession free from encumbrances at the price of £2/5 It is witnessed that in consideration of the said sum of £275 paid by the said John Woods to the said William Boxhal He the said William Boxhal did thereby grant unto the said John Woods and his heirs All and singular the lands and hereditaments mentioned and described in the 1st and 2nd Schedules hereto and hereto with their appurtenances To hold unto and to the use of the said John Woods his heirs and assigns for ever The now-memorialising Indenture and the due execution thereof by the said William Boxhal is witnessed by Frank Mendes Stone of Perth in the Colony aforesaid Solicitor And the same is hereby required to be registered by Arthur Grimsay of Perth aforesaid Law Clerk As witness his hand this 16th day of February 1892

Signed in the presence

Alfred Elbert
Regr of Deeds

Arthur Grimdy
Law Clerk
Perth

The Schedule
Referred to
All that piece or parcel of land situate in the Melbourne District containing 40 acres more or less being Melbourne

Memorial registering the sale of William Boxhal's land to John Woods.

It is not known the precise time that Boxhal moved from the farm, taking all the furniture, and rented a house in Guildford, or when he employed a house keeper, Jane Eyre, to care for his two daughters and for him in his declining health. The loss of Thomas as a worker on the property could have prompted the move. During this time, John Woods kept pressure on him to sell.

At about the time of his move to Guildford, he had a conflict with his daughter, Catherine, similiar to that with Matilda. Catherine, who was then only 17, wanted to marry William Herbert Jacques, the son of a former convict Paul Jacques, who had come on the *Pyrenees* on 28 June 1851. (5) The dispute was not so much her age, but the fact that Jacques was not a Catholic. Boxhal opposed the marriage.

Catherine like her sister Matilda was a "chip off the old block", with a stubborn will and unshakable determination. She was banished when she went to Toodyay and married Jacques in the Good Templars Hall by the Methodist Minister Joseph Mitchell on 2 January 1892.(5a) In a way this was salt in Boxhal's wound because it was in the old Convict Depot where he was sent 36 years earlier.

It is not known whether it was the dispute over Catherine's marriage or the continued pressure from John Woods, that within a month of the marriage, Boxhal agreed to sell his freehold land, Melbourne Locations 383, 102 and 77 to Woods for an agreed total price of 550 pounds. (6) The transfer was arranged by the solicitor F. M. Stone in Perth on 16 February 1892. A conservative estimate is that the amount of money was equivelent to about $250,000 at the time of writing. In cash terms and in relation to his peers, Boxhal was a very rich man.

Almost all material wealth and poverty are inherited, but there are exceptions. These exceptions are rare and usually the result of chance or because the inheritor has outstanding ability and exercises that ability. William Boxhal was born into poverty and inherited poverty and was then subjected to a period of intense privation. Yet, because he had the intellect to assess the situations in which he was placed, the strength to rise above brutality and the ability to work hard, he was one of the exceptions. He had achieved status and far more material wealth than ninety five percent of all the convicts who came to Western Australia.

Despite his wealth, he was saddened by a further tragedy, the death of his fifteen year old daughter, Mary Ann on 16 October,1892.

He was also a sick man and the gradually worsening symptoms were diagnosed as cancer, which at that time was untreatable. The prognosis was that he would soon die. With such certainty he approached a Perth solicitor, J. C. Foulkes to prepare his last Will and Testament.

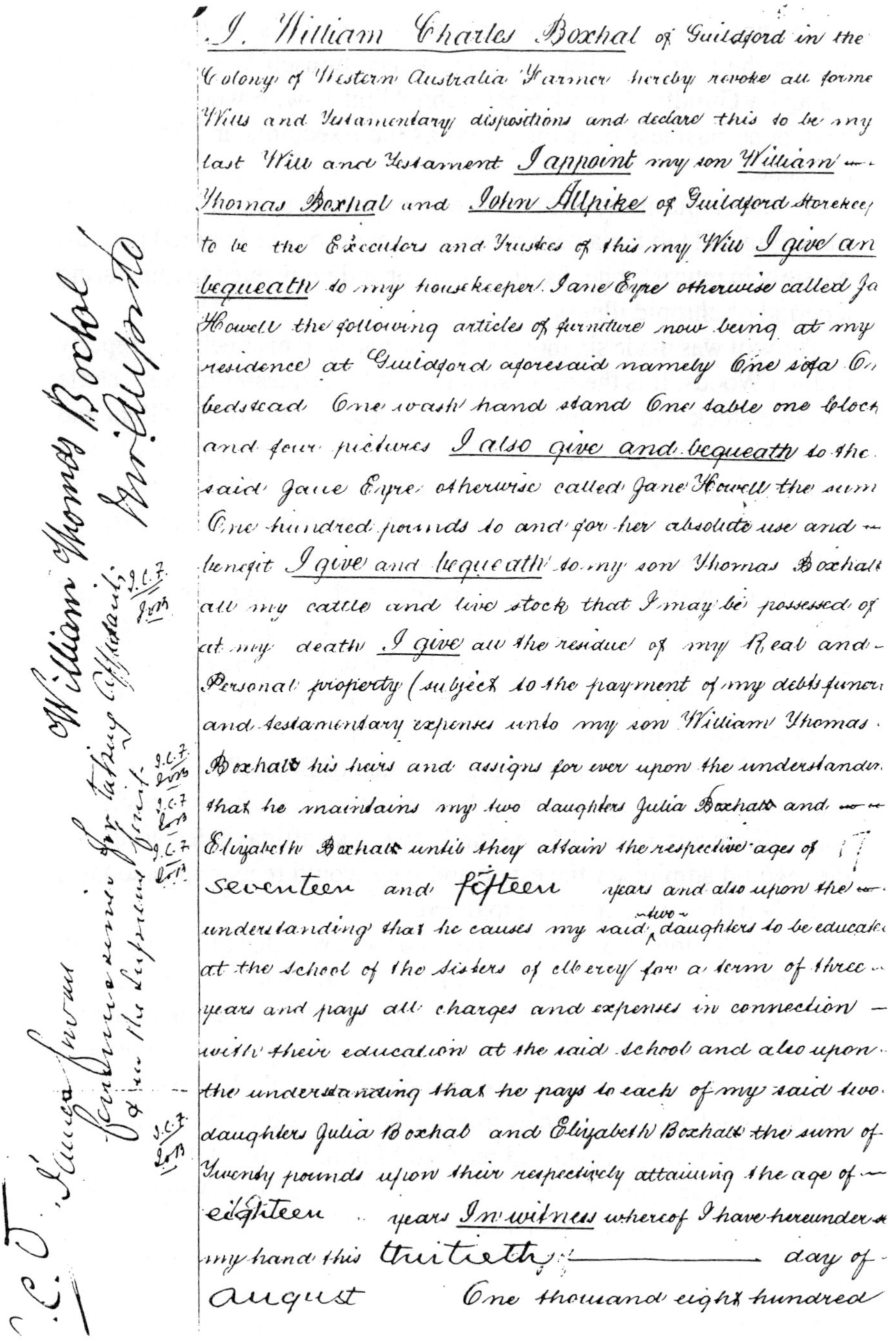

I. William Charles Boxhal of Guildford in the Colony of Western Australia Farmer hereby revoke all former Wills and Testamentary dispositions and declare this to be my last Will and Testament *I appoint my son William Thomas Boxhal* and *John Allpike* of Guildford Storekeeper to be the Executors and Trustees of this my Will *I give and bequeath* to my housekeeper Jane Eyre otherwise called Jane Howell the following articles of furniture now being at my residence at Guildford aforesaid namely One sofa One bedstead One wash hand stand One table one block and four pictures *I also give and bequeath* to the said Jane Eyre otherwise called Jane Howell the sum One hundred pounds to and for her absolute use and benefit *I give and bequeath* to my son Thomas Boxhall all my cattle and live stock that I may be possessed of at my death *I give* all the residue of my Real and Personal property (subject to the payment of my debts funeral and testamentary expenses unto my son William Thomas Boxhall his heirs and assigns for ever upon the understanding that he maintains my two daughters Julia Boxhall and Elizabeth Boxhall until they attain the respective ages of 17 **seventeen** and **fifteen** years and also upon the understanding that he causes my said two daughters to be educated at the school of the Sisters of Mercy for a term of three years and pays all charges and expenses in connection with their education at the said school and also upon the understanding that he pays to each of my said two daughters Julia Boxhal and Elizabeth Boxhall the sum of Twenty pounds upon their respectively attaining the age of **eighteen** years *In witness* whereof I have hereunder set my hand this **thirtieth** ———————— day of **August** One thousand eight hundred

(margin, written vertically)
William Thomas Boxhal
Mr Allpike

C. T. Sharpe Sworn
Acknowledges by taking Affidavit
& see the Deponent sign

The last Will and Testament of William Boxhal,
which he signs as William Charles Boxhal.

95

He appointed his son William (whom he names William Thomas and for the first time that we know, named himself William Charles) (7) and a Guildford storekeeper, John Allpike -with whom he would have done business over the years- as the Executors and Trustees of his estate.

He left the furniture in his house at Guildford to his house- keeper, Jane Eyre and left her a very generous bequest of one hundred pounds, possibly in return for her having cared for and ministered to him during a period of chronic illness.

The will was made six months after he had sold his freehold property to John Woods. It is therefore strange that he bequeaths all his " cattle and live stock " to his son Thomas and "the residue of his "Real and Personal property" to his son William Thomas. This would seem to indicate that Thomas had all the livestock, but no land on which to keep them and William has no land (other than the 3000 acre lease), but no live stock.

William was given the responsibility of maintaining Julia and Elizabeth until their respective ages of 17 and 15 and that "he causes them to be educated at the school of the Sisters of Mercy for a term of three years". He also had to "pay to each of them the sum of twenty pounds ... upon attaining the age of eighteen years".

There is no way of ascertaining the value of Boxhal's assets or how much stock he owned. When probate was declared after his death, his son William and John Allpike simply swore an affidavit declaring that they would administer the estate and they would render an account if and when they were required to do so.

An illustration of Boxhal's strength of will was that although a very sick man and suffering pain he wanted to go back to the place he had lived. Even though the road north from Guildford was much better than earlier times, the journey by horse and buggy would have been long, hot and difficult for a sick man close to death. It is more likely that he would have travelled by train on the railway built by the Midland Railway Company, which had reached Mogumber by 1892.

Michael Lanigan had secured the mail contract from Mogumber to Berkshire Valley. It was much easier for Boxhal to take the train from Guildford, travelling through Midland Junction and Gingin and then going on to Berkshire Valley in Lanigan's mail coach.

He had a desire to see his sons and would have visited William and the Fitzgerald family at Yamarah and then proceed on to the Benedictine Monastery at New Norcia to see the aged Bishop Salvado, his friend

Father Martinez and others. Thomas was working at Berkshire Valley north-east of New Norcia at the old Clinch property.

This was to be William Boxhal's last journey. He died at Berkshire Valley on 12 January 1893 at the age of 61 (8). His body was taken back to New Norcia where Father Martinez buried him with Mary Ann at the Cemetery on 14 January 1893.(9)

Notes:

(1) New Norcia baptismal records, 2953 A / 28.
(2) Rica Erickson and Gillian O'Mara, *Convicts in Western Australia 1850 - 1887, Dictionary of Western Australia, Vol XI,* University of Western Australia Press, Nedlands,1994.
(3) Birth Certificate.
(4) New Norcia Marriage Records.
(5) Erickson & O'Mara, *op. cit.*
(5a) Marriage Certificate, Registrar of Marriages, Perth, 22/1892
(6) Transfer of Land, 242/1892 and Memorial, X1.516.
(7) A reasonable assumption is that the names may have been given when they were confirmed.
(8) Death Certificate, 104/1893. The date of death on the Death Certificate is 15 January and the date of burial is 14 January. As Thomas was illiterate it is more likely that the burial date signed by Father Martinez is correct.
(9) New Norcia burial records, 258.

Catherine Boxhal. She married William Henry Jacques in 1892 and died of tuberculosis at the Wooroloo Sanitorium in 1920, aged 46 years.

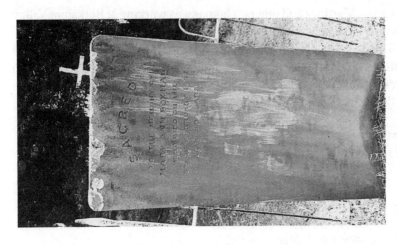

The grave of Mary Ann Boxhal.

The grave of Julia Maher, a daughter of William and Mary Ann Boxhal at New Norcia.

Afterword

What I have written is only a brief history of a man who came from the poverty of England in the nineteenth century, suffered the degradation of incarceration on a Hulk in the Thames and transportation to the depressed Swan River Colony in Western Australia, where he performed hard physical labour.

Despite all this, his spirit was not broken. He overcame a harsh climate and tamed the Australian bush without capital; he purchased land, became a successful farmer and raised a family of eight children.

He, like many other former convicts, helped to save the colony from economic decline and those that survived added a unique and valuable dimension to the colony; but his legacy to Western Australia truly resides in his many law abiding descendants.

There were those who served and died in the armed forces in both world wars. Boxhal's first three grandsons (whom he may not have met) were the children of Matilda and Henry Playford, George Henry Playford, born 12 February 1890 and Alfred Charles, Playford, born 23 December 1891and their cousin, Robert William Boxhal, the son of Thomas and Alice Boxhal, born 27 July 1893, all served in the AIF in the first World War.

The first to enlist was the younger Playford who joined the 28th Battalion in 1915 with the regimental number 2431 and saw action at Gallipoli near the end of the campaign. The 28th Battalion, which was part of the 7th Brigade, fought with valour in France in several notable battles. Alfred Playford was seriously wounded, possibly in the second battle of Bullecourt, which took place in May 1917, where many of the Battalion were killed or wounded. He was transferred to the 51st Battalion and repatriated to Australia on the *Nestor*, arriving at Fremantle on 13 September 1917. He was discharged on 23 October 1917. For a time he received a war pension, but during the Second World War he enlisted in the Provost Corp on 25 July 1940. He was promoted to the rank of corporal on 11 November 1940, but was discharged on 27 June 1941. He died in Perth on 27 June 1952.

Robert Boxhal and his cousin George Playford both joined the 44th Battalion at about the same time (Boxhal's Regimental number was

894 and Playford's 933).(1) It is possible that they may not have known each other or their relationship before enlisting. Boxhal grew up near New Norcia and Gillingarra and Playford in South Perth. Boxhal was in the Machine Gun section of the Battalion and Playford was attached to H.Q. Company. Both had the rank of transport driver, which is most likely a recognition of their horsemanship. They left Fremantle with the first contingent of the 44th Battalion on the H.M.A.T *Suevic* on 6 June 1916, "leaving behind the biggest crowd of people that had ever assembled on the West Australian waterfront". (2)

After training in the Middle East and England, the Battalion first engaged its major action in France at the battle of Messines, which commenced on 7 June 1917. (3) There were a series of patrols before the main offensive on Messines and the German artillery bombarded the Australians. On 1 June Robert Boxhal and two close friends, Drivers William McNeece and William Short "were all killed by one shell".(4) He was 23 years of age and is buried in the Strand Military Cemetery at Comines-Warneton, Hainault in Belguim.(5)

George Playford received serious injuries and mustard gas poisoning when he was trapped under a dead horse in a shell-hole for three days. He was invalided back to England. The drama of his rescue resulted in him receiving a letter from King George V which read:

> The Queen and I wish you God-speed and a safe return to your home and dear ones.
>
> A grateful Mother Country is proud of your splendid service, characterised by unsurpassed devotion and courage.
>
> Signed George RI

With the war coming to an end and following his recovery in England, George Playford had a wild time going absent without leave on three seperate occasions for a total of 63 days, returning nine days after armistice on 20 November 1918. He served 60 days "F.P." and returned to Australia in the *City of York*, arriving in Fremantle on 18 February 1919. (6) George Playford came from tough stock. After his discharge in April 1919 and despite his ordeal he led an active hard-working life until he died of cancer on 10 March 1944.

In the second World War, George Heny Playford's son, (also) George Henry, joined the Royal Australian Air Force as a radar mechanic soon after his eighteenth birthday in 1944 and served until April 1946.

W.X. 5286
Sgt. J. F. Kehoe

40 18
41 19
42 20
43 21

Geprüft
Stalag XVIII A
89

26/5/44

Mr & Mrs M. Kehoe
36. 10th avenue
Maylands.
Feb 29th '44

My Darling John.

We have just had the first news of you today Mary got your card, dated 24th Oct I have not had any letter from you since before the surrender of Italy. I have written 3 letters to you, and addressed them to Stalagg 344. Mrs Smith had word that her son, Wally, was in Stalagg 344 as he had been in Camp 57, I thought you may be with him in Germany. Des has been in Canada for some months and has recieved a commission. He is P/O. He told me he had a letter from you. He arranged to send you tobacco. I also got Boans to send you tobacco from a firm in England. I sent 4 clothing parcels while you were in Italy. one parcel had a pair of boots. Des is back in England, by now. He had his 20th birthday in England & his 21st in Canada. Poor old Kev is still in the parts. He is a Flight. Sgt. In one of my letters I told you that Kev got married. He was home from Townsville on an embarkation leave so they got married. They had a lovely marriage with Nuptial Mass. Carmel looked very nice. On Nov 3rd they got married. Well, while we always have these pleasant and happy events, there is

---

Letter of Mrs Margaret Kehoe, the grandaughter of William Boxhal, to her son John Kehoe who was a German prisoner of war, 29 February 1944.
(Courtesy of Mr John Francis Kehoe)

always some sad things and sorrows in many homes, but when God wills these things, we must bow to His Will. A week after Kev's wedding, Aunty Ciss died at the early age of 46 in Queensland. We all need to be brave. I, with all my boys away so far from me, and in danger had to face things with a strong will. Who could be braver than your own dear self. I know when I tell you that our darling Austin has gone to join the ranks of God, instead of the ranks of an earthly soldier. God that you will be brave. God saw fit to call him to Himself. He died of Malaria in N.G. on Feb 14th '44 one of the best & loved by all. I regret having to tell you this but we could not let you come home not knowing about it. The anxiety of not knowing where you were, & then this blow, may be imagined and still I am here, so now my darling be like one able to say. Not thy will but Thine dear Lord. Pray for him Johnny dear. May his dear soul R.I.P. My page is nearly full. I am thankful to know where you are. The wonderful news lightened my burdened shoulders. I will send a parcel straight away & some tobacco. Father Dunne & everybody have been so good to us. Will write more soon, with plenty of prayers & Masses for you my dear one, I will close & hope you'll soon be home. Best love From Your

all fairly well   loving Mum

Four sons of Maggie Boxhal, who married Daniel O'Connell Kehoe, served with distinction in the second World War. The eldest of the four, John Francis Kehoe (WX 5268), who was born 3 December 1915, joined the 2nd 28th Battalion, which was part of the AIF 9th Division that fought with great gallantry at Tobruk and El Alamein. He survived the fury of Rommell's "Afrika Korps" artillery and Stuka bombardment and the eight month's of freezing cold and blazing heat in the 1941 seige of Tobruk. During the strategically important battle at El Alamein the 28th Battalion suffered "the greatest losses...in its attack on Ruin Ridge" on 18 July 1942. Sergent John Kehoe and 488 members of the Battalion were taken prisoner by the Germans. This was in addition to the 946 other Australians of the 9th Division who were captured.(7) He was one of several thousand crammed into a ship and transported from Bengazi to Brendisi in Italy. He spent the rest of the War as prisoner of war in Austria in Stalag XV111A.

Keven Redmond Kehoe, who was born 23 March 1917, joined the Royal Australian Air Force and served as a Wireless Operater/Air Gunner in the No. 8 Squadron, flying Beaufort Bombers in New Guinea and Rabaul. He was discharged with the rank of Warrant Officer from No.35 Squadron in June 1945.

Joseph Austin Kehoe, who was born 14 September 1918 was a member of the 30th Battalion of the A.I.F. He held the rank of Warrant Officer when he died in action in New Guinea at the age of 25 on 14 February 1944. He is buried in the Lae War Cemetery in Papua New Guinea.(8)

The youngest of the Kehoe brothers, Desmond Noel, who was born 26 December 1923, was a Flying Officer, pilot (415429) with the No. 462 Squadron of the Royal Australian Air Force. Nearing the end of the war, after numerous bombing missions, his Halifax bomber and three others from the squadron were shot down over Germany. Kehoe and all, but one, of the seven in his crew were killed on 24 February 1945.(9) He was 21 Years of age and was buried in the Reichwald Forest War Cemetery, south west of Kleve in Germany.(10)

Carmel Kehoe, a sister of the Kehoe brothers served as a member of the Australian Women's Army Service as a gunner, attached to the Albany Fixed Defence Command Post.(11)

Allan Francis Hogan, who was born 8 April 1924, was a cousin of the Kehoes and the son of Ellen Mary Boxhal and Herbert Hogan. He joined the Royal Australian Air Force soon after his eighteenth birthday. He was a pilot with the No. 460 Squadron stationed at Binbook in Lancashire, England and flew 26 missions over Germany in Lancaster bombers. He was discharged on 5 October 1945 with the rank of Flying Officer.

During the Korean War, John Greenhill, who was the grandson of Julia Boxhal, joined the Royal Australian Navy and served on HMAS *Australia* and on HMAS *Melbourne* during the Malaya campaign. He was discharged in 1958 while stationed at HMAS *Harman*.

Western Australian society is enriched today by the accomplishments and enterprise of many hundreds of Boxhal's progeny. While it is not possible to identify all or prudent to name only some, there are many who have become successful farmers, police officers, business managers, accountants, civil servants, builders, tradesmen, bankers and journalists.

Despite what was a poor or nonexistent formal education of the first generation of Boxhal's family, many in the present generation have achieved high academic success. There are many scholars and graduates in the judiciary, medicine, engineering, dentistry, psychology, education, science, commerce, law and the arts.

In the field of sport there have been representatives of State and Country to the level of the Olympic Games.

Notes:

(1) C.Longmore, *Eggs-A-Cook,* Coulortype Press Ltd.,Perth. pp.198 and 199.
(2) C.Longmore op.cit. p.8.
(3) C.E.W. Bean *The Official History of Australia in the War of 1914-1918 Volume IV. The A.I.F. in France.* University of Queensland Press.1931 p. 587.
(4) C. Longmore op. sit. p.38.
(5) Commonwealth War Graves Commission. Grave reference: 11.D.5.
(6) Army pay book, George Henry Playford 6 June 1916 - 4 April 1919.
(7) Barton Maughan, *Australia in the War 1939-1945, Tobruk and El Alamein*, Canberra Australian War Memorial, 1966.p.755.
(8) Commonwealth War Graves Commission. Grave reference: JJ.C.10.
(9) John Herington, *Air Power over Europe 1944-1945 Canberra* Australian War Memorial, 1963.
(10) Commonwealth War Graves Commission. Grave reference: 31.A.5.
(11) Australian War Memorial Photograph Database. Women, Coastal defences; 1939-1945. No.029644.

Genealogy

Information on the decendents of William Boxhal has been sought from many who have kindly responded. The author has numerous dedicated people to thank for their diligent research, especially Barbara Mitting the grand daughter of Catherine Boxhal and Walter Herbert Jacques, Patricia Cole, the grand daughter of William Boxhal and Ellen Mary Fitzgerald and Sheila Drew, the grand daughter of Julia Boxhal and Richard Maher.

Great care has been taken to ensure accuracy, but mistakes can happen. The information on the extended Boxhal family has been sought to make it as comprehensive as possible. If there are errors or ommissions the author can only apologise. Some of the early dates of birth are likely to be baptismal dates, rather than the actual dates of birth With the exception of the first generation, the spelling of the surname of Boxhal varies in the recovered documents. The spelling used in this genealogy is Boxhal, which is used in the body of the book.

Thomas Boxhal married 11 April 1831 **Matilda Fegent**
b. 25 December 1809   b.14 August 1814 Eashing,
 Surrey England   Surrey, England
d. 5 May 1846 Lewisham,
Kent, England

Children

William Boxhal
b.12 February 1832 Eashing Surrey England.

Eunice Boxhal
b.5 January1834 Eashing Surrey England.

Juliana Boxhal
b.28 June 1835 Eashing Surrey England.

Mary Ann Boxhal
b. 11 December 1837 Eashing Surrey England.
d.20 December 1837 Eashing Surrey England.

Matilda Boxhal
b. 10 March 1839 Camberwell, London, England.

Henry Boxhal
b. 8 August 1841 Croydon, Surrey, England

Thomas Boxhal
b. 5 November 1843 Croydon, Surrey, England

Alfred Boxhal
b. 13 August 1845 Deptford, Kent, England

William Boxhal   married 4 May 1863 Perth **Mary Ann Kelly**
b.12 February 1832 Eashing Surrey, b. 2 March 1847 Umballa, India.
           England
d. 15 January 1893 Berkshire Valley,   d. 3 February 1887 New Norcia,
       Western Australia   Western Australia.

Children

William Thomas Boxhal
b. 13 June 1864.
d. 13 July 1951

Matilda Catherine Boxhal
b. 15 May 1866.
d. 15 September 1930

Joanna Boxhal
b. 31 January 1868.
d. 8 May 1868.

Thomas Joseph Boxhal
b. 9 November 1869.
d. 8 June 1954

Catherine Boxhal
b. 15 May 1874.
d. 1 May 1920

Mary Ann Boxhal
b. 16 October 1876
d. 1892

Julia Ann Boxhal
b. 21 December 1878.
d.13May 1967

Elizabeth Mary Boxhal
b. 26 November 1881.
d.

Ellen Boxhal
b. 22 August 1886.
d. 1 January 1887.

The line of William Boxhal jnr

William Boxhal   married 16 September 1884. **Ellen Mary Fitzgerald**
b. 13 June 1864.   b. 1 August 1860.
d. 13 July 1951   d. 21August 1920
Children

Mary Margaret Boxhal married 3 August 1907 **Daniel O'Connell Kehoe**
b. 11 May 1886.   b. 1 August 1864 Ireland
d. 6 September 1949   d. 28 June 1946.
Children
Eugene Joseph Kehoe
b.16 May 1908.

Vivienne MaryKehoe   m. 4 May 1931.   **Gerald Joseph Hogan**
b. 22 June 1909.   23 March 1907.
d 5 May 1990.   8 March 1995
Children

Maureen Anne Hogan   married   **Eric Robert Pearce**
b. 7 August 1932   b. 29 October 1931
Children
Susan Mary Pearce
b. 28 March 1958

Stephen Gerard Pearce married 21 June 1997 **Anna-Marie Charwood**
b. 1 September 1959   b. 25 October 1968

Luke Robert Pearce
b. 24 February 2000

Colleen Margaret Pearce
b.20 December 1961.

Timothy Mark Pearce married. 7 November 1992 **Sarah Jane Bennett**
b. 13 August 1964.   b. 23 May 1968
Children
Madeleine Jane Pearce
b.1 July 1994
Lara Jane Pearce
b. 17 October 1995
Nathan Robert Pearce
b 11 March 2000

Daniel Joseph Pearce married 20 October 1990 **Tracy Louise Pearson**
b. 18 September 1966   b. 13 February 1966
Children
Mitchell Joseph Pearce
b.15 April 1994
Nicholas Jordon Pearce
b.7 November 1995
Thomas Jacob Pearce
b.14 June 1997

Miriam Margaret Hogan married 4 May 1957 **Brian Aiden Peachey**
b. 12 November 1933   b.10 June 1929
Children
Damian Joseph Peachey
b. 18 April 1958

Mary Peachey
b. 21 July 1959
d. 22 July 1959

Catherine Mary Peachey married 30 January 1982 **Paul Michael Cotton**
b.9 July 1960   b. 3 January 1959
Children
Benjamin Paul Cotton
b.23 May 1983

Emily Catherine Cotton
b. 1 June 1985
Katie Elizabeth Cotton
b.28 November 1992

Anne Frances Peachey married 10 July 1988 **David John Clear**
b. 16 August 1962   b. 10 December 1964
Children
Sarah Ellen Clear
b. 8 July 1991
Joseph William Clear
b. 9 March 1994

Jane Marie Peachey married 9 April 1983 **Kenneth Trevor Howells**
b. 31 January 1964   b. 31 July 1958
Children
Matthew Trevor Howells
b. 31 August 1983
Joshua Stephen Howells
b. 7 January 1986

Jacinta Miriam Peachey
b. 14 July 1965

Brendan John Peachey married 16 October 1999 **Nicola Elizabeth Quinlan**
b. 3 October 1968   d. 2 October 1974

Francesca Louise Peachey
b.25 February 1970

Lucy Anne Peachey
b. 15 January 1972

Gwenyth Mary Hogan married 6 February 1960 **Arthur Rudolph White**
b.29 July 1935   b. 1 March 1933
Children
Therese Mary White

Marie Cecelia White   married 18 July 1982   **David Walker**
b. 10 January 1962
Children
Krystal Marie Walker
b. 24 April 1983
2nd marriage   19 September 1992   **Matthew Conrick**
Children
Jessica Louise Conrick
b. 14 May 1995
William Mathew Conrick
b. 28 July 1998

Vincent Paul White
b. 8 August 1963

Edward Joseph White and **Jane Sutherland**
b. 17 July 1965
d.1 October 1998
Children
Leonie Kate White
b.19 December 1997

Robert Arthur White   married 15 March 1997   **Vanessa Joy McOuat**
b. 31 October 1966   b.6 October 1969
Children
Zachary Robert White
b.23 September 1996
Benjamin Michael White
b.13 March 1998

Louis Phillip White
b. 4 October 1968
David Matthew White
b.14 July 1971.
Peter John White
b.14 December 1972.
John Michael White
b.5 December 1977

Barry Joseph Hogan   married 2 May 1964   **Patricia Anne McMahon**
b.16 January 1940   b.22 August 1943
Children
Anthony Joseph Hogan
b. 13 August 1965.
Mark Edward Hogan   married 3 April 1998   **Romaine Michelle Oliver**
b. 3 December 1969   b.19 August 1965
Children
Corey James Hogan
b.13 April 1992
Nastassia Tess Hogan
b. 27 January 1994

Gerard Daniel Kehoe
b.1911

Mary Patricia Kehoe   m. 25 September 1937   **Leonard Henry Mc Ouat**
b. 7 June1913   b. 12 December 1910
d. 19 September 1995   d. 6 January 1995
Children
Garry Leonard McOuat   married   **Diana Joy Wilson**
b.29 November 1938   b.8 December 1940
Children
Vanessa Joy McOuat   married 15 March 1997   **Robert Arthur White**
b.6 October 1969   31 October 1969
Children
Samantha Joy
b.1 December 1990
Zachary Robert White
b.23 September 1996
Benjamin Michael White
b.13 March 1998

Annette Patricia McOuat   married   **Kevin Meredith Carton**
b.8 May 1940   b. 26 October 1933
Children
Romilly Anne Carton
b.26 March 1961.
Jeremy Kevin Carton   married   **Julie Ellen Kalinowski**
b.21 July 1962   b. 16 December 1963
Children
Luke Oliver Carton
b.24 January 1992
Daniel Connor Carton
b.15 December 1993
Ella Patricia Carton
b. 7 November 1998
Timothy Andrew Carton
b.25 June 1967

Margaret Grace McOuat   married   **Lance Thomas Twomey**
b. 20 August 1942   b.10 November 1940
Children
Clare Margaret Twomey   married   **Gary Emblen**
b.24 April 1965   b.1960
Children
Jack Emblen
b. 9 September 1992

Christopher Mark Twomey
b.1 October 1966
Children
Tarrin Twomey
22 February 1992

Luke James Twomey
b.11 February 1972

Bruce Daniel McOuat
b.24 March 1944

Jocelyn Mary McOuat	married	**Keith Richardson**
b.4 May 1953		b. 8 October 1951

Children
Scott Richardson
b.20 August 1977
Brad Richardson
b.12 December 1979
Todd Richardson
b.13 July 1981

Raymond George McOut
b. 4 May1953

<u>Hillary Kehoe</u>

<u>Edward Kehoe</u>

<u>John Francis Kehoe</u>	married 1947	**Delores Josephine McAdam**
b. 3 December 1915		b.
		d.1 August 1989

Children
Desmond Francis Kehoe
b.2 August 1959

Jonine Frances Kehoe	married	**John Francis Milbourne**
b.13 December 1960		

Children
Ella Frances Milbourne
b1991

<u>Kevin Redmond Kehoe</u>	married 1943	**Carmel Mary Clohessy**
b.23 March 1917		b.4 November 1920

Children
Mary Therese Kehoe	married 14 April 1972	**David Jeffery**
b. 24 June 1946		b.11 November 1945

Michael Joseph Kehoe
b.22 December 1947
Daniell John Kehoe
b.4 March 1950
Children
Joel Quinn
b.7 February 1989

Anne Frances Kehoe	married 22 March 1987	**William T Coleman**
b. 8 January 1954		b.22 July 1943

Children
Nichole Jane Coleman
b. 16 January 1989

b. 16 January 1989
Joseph Austin Kehoe
b. 14 September 1918
d 14 February 1944, New Guinea.

Carmel Constance Kehoe   married 1946   Francis McAdam
b. 11 August 1920   b. 16 June 1918
d. 1 June 1991   d. 24 June 1995
Children
Barbara Carmel McAdam   married 8 May 1971   Jeremiah (Dermot) Tuohy
b. 4 November 1946   b.30 September 1946
Children
Justin Tuohy   married 9 January 1999   Jan Simone Meuzelaar
b.1 August 1972   b.20 July 1972
Tyrone Francis Tuohy
b. 23 February 1974
Penelope Barbara Tuohy
b. 15 October 1979
Rosemary Carmel Tuohy
b. 23 November 1979
   d. 19 July 1998
Josephine Teresa Tuohy
b.31 July 1983
Kathleen Maree Tuohy
b.4 January 1987

Austin Francis McAdam married 13 November 1971 Josephine Lambertina
b. 17 January 1948   (Margot) Veltman
                                                b.17 May 1951

 Children
Marlee Jane McAdam
b.17 August 1974
Matthew Francis McAdam
b.28 January 1977
Travis Austin McAdam
b.30 August 1978

Jennifer Margaret McAdam married 22 April 1972 Desmond John Hollis
b.27 March 1950   b. 14 October 1949
Children
Virginia Clare Hollis
b. 15 June 1978
Courtney Desmond Hollis
b.14 October 1983

Imelda Bernadette McAdam married 13 May 1972 Peter Charles Cooper
b. 7 August 1951   b. 13 September 1951
Children
Meg Carmel Cooper
b. 28 May 1976
Laurence Charles Cooper

Jonathon Peter Cooper
b.17 December 1983

Desmond Noel Kehoe
b.26 February 1923
d. 23 February 1945, Germany.

Terance O'Connel Kehoe
b.1925

Mary Ann Boxhal	married 1909	**George Chitty**
b. 5 July 1888		b.1880
d. 5 May 1948		d. 22 April 1959

Children

Evangeline Lucy Chitty	married	**Henry James Forward**
b.30 December 1909		d. 24 April 1974

George William Chitty
b. 7 September 1911
Bridget Mary Chitty
b.8 November 1913
William George Chitty
b.1914
d. 17 December 1988
Maxwell Claude Chitty
b. 1918
d. 15 March 1974
Douglas Chitty
b. 1920

Marie Terese Chitty	married	**J Williams**
b.1922		
d. 17 January 1978		

CatherineMary Boxhal	married 7 January 1914	**William Milford Weston**
b. 28 September 1890		
d. 11 November 1937		d.20 March 1958

Children

Alyce Veronica (Vera) Weston	married 27 October 1941	**Bernard Hodges**
b.10 July 1914		
d.15 August 1985		

Children

John Bernard Hodges	married 9 January 1971	**Lyn Pike**
b. 25 June 1947		

Children
Malcolm John Hodges
b. 5 August 1975
Leanne Michelle Hodges
b. 26 May 1978

Geoffery William Hodges
b. 25 November 1949
d. 9 September 1996

Lindsay Grant Hodges married 5 February 1977 **Norma Robson**
b. 2 January 1952
Children
Tanya Joanne
b. 25 March 1979

Judith Alison Hodges married 12 April 1975 **Peter Goodby**
b. 14 October 1954
Children
Scott William Goodby
b.1 June 1977
Naree Alyce Goodby
b. 31 July 1979

<u>Leslie William Weston</u>
b.15 June 1916
d. 29 August 1982

<u>Milford Warren Weston</u> married 30 March 1942 **Jean Doreen Cordon**
b. 19 January 1918   b. 6 October 1822
d. 26 November 1981   d.
Children
Lynette Jean Weston married 9 January 1965 **Kevin Desmond Clune**
b. 16 march 1943   b.29 November 1936
Children
Michael Francis Clune married 19 March 1994 **Stacye Rochelle Bennett**
b.13 march 1968
Denise Marie Clune married 28 October 1995 **Gary Thomas Jones**
b.31 March 1971
Children
Rowan William
1 July 1998

Graeme John Weston married 14 August 1976 **Robyn Russo**
b.7 September 1944   b. 22 November 1944
Children
Shane Anthony Weston
b. 22 February 1979

Catherine Mary Weston married 5 August 1972 **Gerhard Leopold Dietrich**
b. 30 October 1952   b.26 November 1952
Children
Janine Marie Dietrich
b. 19 February 1976'
Clare Louise Dietrich
b. 13 April 1978

Peter Milford Weston married 1 September 1990 **Dorinda Mary Oppel**
b. 6 September 1955   b.13 October 1959
Children
Amy Alison Weston
b. 16 June 1993

Laura Brooke Weston
b. 14 february 1996

Jennifer Ann Weston   married 8 October 1977   **Harold Bond Neil**
b.29 December 1957   b.22 April 1955
Children
Glen Anthony Neil
b.27 May 1982
Shane Phillip Neil
b. 10 November 1984

Anne Marie Weston   married 27 March 1988   **Dale Wilhelm Nylander**
b.19 June 1960   b. 26 November 1955
Children
Jay Wilhelm Nylander
b.18 November 1990

Anthony Francis Weston married 13 March 1982   **Lynda Sutton**
b. 4 October 1961   b. 3 December 1960
Children
Jessica Leigh Weston
b. 1985
Matthew Gordon Weston
b. 8 October 1987
David Anthony Weston
b. 22 June 1989

Julie Elizabeth Weston   married 14 March 1993   **David Evans**
b.19 November 1964   b. 1 April 1963

<u>**Cecilia Mary Boxhal**</u>   married 1922   **Henry G Thomson**
b. 7 February 1898
d.   1943
Children
Norma Thomson
<u>**Cecilia Mary Boxhal**</u>   2nd marriage   **Thomas Brennan**

<u>**Ellen Mary Boxhal**</u>   m. April 1923   **Herbert Hogan**
b. 25 April 1900   b. 2 December 1899
d. 6 November 1960   d.16 January 1980
Children
<u>Allan Francis Hogan</u>   married 3 April 1948   **Gleneath Mary Whitely**
b. 8 April 1924   b. 13 May 1925
d.3 September 1996   d.2 July 1972
2nd marriage **Pauline Beatrice Sachse**
b. 25 July 1936
Children
Terrence Joseph Hogan   married   **Carolyn Anne Gardner**
b.29 February 1952   b. 20 February 1956
Children
Martin Warwick Hogan
b.17 March 1987

Elizabeth Ellen Hogan
b.21 May 1991

Patrick John Hogan   married 5 June 1982   **Julee Jack Bently**
b. 23 March 1953   b.5 November 1957
Children
Lisa Maree Hogan
b. 15 April 1985
Kimberlee Helen Hogan
b. 6 July 1987
Sean Patrick Hogan
b. 24 September 1990

Martin Gerard Hogan   married 12 May 1984   **Deborah Lorraine Neller**
b.13 March 1956   b.20 November 1956

Jovita Mary Hogan   married   **William Alec Wilson**
b. 13 December 1958   b.13 February 1958
Children
Claudia Alec Hogan-Wilson
b. 4 February 1995
Louis Allan Hogan-Wilson
b.16 January 1997

Eileen Mary Hogan   married 29 January 1983   **Colin Disley**
b.12 January 1962   b. 12 May 1959
d. 31 October 1997

<u>Patricia Elizabeth Hogan</u> married 24 January 1953 **Terence John Cole**
b. 21 February 1932   b. 28 June 1928
Children
John Raymond Cole   married   **Lynn Marie Smith**
b.20 October 1953
Children
Gemma Louise Cole
b. 27 April 1979
Timothy John Cole
b.4 July 1983
Angela Jane Cole
b. 28 August 1986

Stephen Michael Cole   married 4 September 1982 **Donna Currie**
b. 11 May 1955   b. 12 June 1961
Children
Ethan Michael Cole
b.22 July 1991
Jordon Douglas Cole
b.15 June 1994
Kelsi Anne Cole
b. 3 April 1998

Paul Terence Cole   married 14 January 1977 **Joanne Hicks**
b. 11 May 1955   b. 20 February 1954

Children
Elizabeth Amy Cole
b. 27 July 1983
Nicholas David Cole
b.5 September 1985
Thomas Patrick Cole
b. 22 October 1989

Kathryn Patricia Cole	married September 1977	**Shane Patrick Kirwin**
b. 24 December 1956		b. 28 May 1953

Peter Thomas Cole
b. 22 August 1958

Andrew James Cole	married	**Stacey Smart**
b. 20 October 1961		b.6 November 1960

Children
Matthew James Cole
b.20 October 1981

Christina Mary Cole	married	**Robert Batten**
b.15 October 1964		b. 9 January 1955

Children
Rebecca Elizabeth Batten
b.7 October 1995
Jacob Nathaniel Batten
b.7 February 1998

Judith Maxine Hogan	married 1955	**Thomas Francis Redmond Doyle**
b. 26 April 1934		b. 28 August 1933

Children

Anne-Marie Doyle	married 3 January 1981	**Hugh Samuel Strain**
b. 10 April 1959		b.1959

Children
Danielle Lucy Strain
b.23 May 1986
Katherine Sophy Strain
b. 14 June 1989

Anthony Raymond Doyle	married 1 April 1995	**Pia Hewitt**
b. 10 November 1962		

Children
Rose Mary Francis Doyle
b. 14 February 1996
Luke Thomas Doyle
b. 15 January 1998

The line of Matilda Catherine Boxhal

Matilda Catherine Boxhal married 24 April 1889   **Henry Playford**
b. 15 May 1866   b. 26 June 1867
d.15 September 1930   d 5 June 1938.
Children
George Henry Playford   married 13 July 1925   **Beatrice Ormsby Reston**
b. 12 February 1890   b.30 July 1891
d. 10 March 1944   d. 8 September 1937
Children
George Henry Playford married 24 September 1966 **Joan Hazel Mead**
b. 18 February 1926   b.27 November 1936
Children
George Henry Playford
b.16 July 1969
Brent William Playford
b.3 January 1972

Alfred Charles Playford
b. 23 December 1891
d. 10 June 1952

Sarah Anne Playford
b.4 March 1894
d.18 April 1894

The line of Thomas Joseph Boxhal

Thomas Joseph Boxhal   married 30 April 1890   **Alice Thompson**
b. 9 November 1869   b. 8 July 1864
d.8 June 1954   d. 20 June 1940

Children
Mary Ann Margaret Boxhal
b. January 1891
d. 13 December 1893

Robert William Boxhal
b.27 July 1893
d 1 June 1917 France

Margaret Mary Boxhal
b. 30 December 1895
d. 16 October 1982

Ellen Patricia Boxhal
b. 16 March 1898
d. 20 January 1900

Patrick James Boxhal
b. 5 November 1900
d. 9 September 1983

Mary Ann Boxhal
b. 30 April 1901
d.

Mary Ellen Boxhal   married 1929   **Frederick J Thompson**
b. 30 April 1905

                                                d. 15 March 1985

The line of Catherine Boxhal

Catherine Boxhal   married 2 January 1892   **Walter Herbert Jacques**
b.9 December 1874   b. 11 April 1869.
d. 1 May 1920   d. 23 May 1939.

Children

Matilda Elizabeth Jacques married 11 June 1914 **Arthur John Edwards**
b. 6 October 1892   b.1884
d. 24 April 1924   d. 2 January 1924
Children
Leslie Herbert John Edwards married 7 July 1945 **Elsie Irene Kiddie**
b. 16 October 1914   b.6 July 1924
Children
John David Edwards
b,11 November 1946
Jean Edwards   married 1975   **Stephen Cracket**
b. 13 March 1951
Children
Spencer Cracket
November 1976
Shaun Cracket
Dean Cracket

Julia Catherine Jacques
b. 1 November 1895.
d. 5 February 1968.

Maud Margaret Jacques
b.30 April 1897
d.29 June 1897.

Susan Ann Jacques   married 23 October 1918 **Robert Duncan Quinn**
b. 1 July 1898   b. 4 July 1878
d. 4 February 1932   d. 6 May 1953
Children
Susan May Catherine Mary Quinn
b. 1919
d.5 May 1920

Gladys Susan Quinn married 4 December 1943 **Lawrence Edward Hedington**
b. 4 August 1921.
Children
Graham LawrenceHedington married 17 February 1968 **Margaret Scarr**
b.14 August 1945   b.15 August 1946

Yvonne G Hedington married 16 November 1968 **Gary M Jeavons**
20 December 1948

Children
Naomi Jeavons
Simone Jeavons
Ashley Jeavons

Pamela J Hedington   married 1975   **Bruce J James**
18 May 1950   b 25 May 1947
Children
Travis James
Scott James
Reece James

Robert Walter Michael Quinn   married 1951   **Laurel Hoddy**
b30 January 1923
d. 22 June 1985
Children
Susan Rose Quinn
Ian Quinn
Rodney Quinn

Fanny Amy Quinn   married 10 October 1947 **Thomas Heil**
b.30 December 1928
 2nd marriage **Victor Thomas**
Children
Malcolm Heil married 27 April 1916
b.20 April 1948 .

Martha Louise Jacques   married 1935   **William Harry Dixon**
b.2 February 1901   b. 31 December 1886
d. 23 October 1943   d. 4 October 1943
Children
Arthur John Dixon
b.1925
d.2 October 1960
Shirley Josephine Dixon married 22 August 1955 **Frank Eatwell**
17 December 1936
Children
Steven Eatwell
b.3 February 1956
Jeffrey Eatwell
b.25 January 1958
David Eatwell
b. 22 October 1960
d. 9January 1976
Mark Eatwell
b.12 May 1962
Gregory John Eatwell
b. 3 August 1964
d. 3 August 1964
Tammy Eatwell
b.9 September 1966

Kelly May Eatwell
b.31 December 1973
d, 31 december 1973

Lydia May Jacques   married 14 July 1934   **Thomas Comb**
b. 3 August 1903   b. 3 May 1905
d. 24 May1983   d. 23 October 1973.
Children
David Charles Comb   married 2 September1960   **Pamela Mary Kenneywell**
b.2 September 1936   b. 7 November 1937
Children
Michelle Comb
b.13 April 161
Lisa Antoinette Comb   married19 November 1983   **Alan Ray**
b. 7 December 1962   b.4 September 1952
Children
James Ray
b.30 November 1985
Amanda Ray
b. 17 August 1988

Peter Comb
   b. June 1971

David Charles Comb   married 28 February 1981   **Joyce Tonkin**
b. 2 September 1936

Barbara Mary Comb   married 24 February 1962   **Alan Edward Mitting**
b.14 September 1942   **b.14 March 1937**
   Children
Paul Rodney Mitting   married 16 February 1991   **Cheryl Ann Robinson**
b.4 March 1964   b. 21 May 1970
Sharlene Gaye Mitting   married 14 April 1990   **William Hume Kennedy**
b.13 October 1965   b. 25 March 1958
Children
Adrian Hume Kennedy
b. 27 June 1991
Andrew Alan Kennedy
b. 19 March 1994
 Glen Andrew Mitting   married 14 February 1998   **Karen Ann Kelly**
b.6 August 1968   b.19 April 1975
Children
Kristofer Michael Kelly Mitting
b. 19 March 1999

Janene Maree Mitting
b.17 December 1970
d. 17 December 1970

Mary Frances Jacques married 13 August 1932   **Joseph Melbourne**
b. 31 January 1907   b. 10 September 1885
d. 25 May 1987   d. 25 October 1971

Children
Valma May Melbourne married 10 September 1955 **Neil Newton**
b. 7 March 1937
d. 30 December 1960
Children
Gary Newton
b. 21 May 1957

Ronald Melbourne   married 5 August 1972   **Norma Fay Cook**
b. 7 January 1938   b. 26 February 1950
Children
Craig Anthony Melbourne
b.2 July 1972
Donna Terese Melbourne
b.18 November 1973
Jamie Ernest Melbourne
b. 11 August 1976
Jodie Valma Melbourne
b. 26 December 1979

Walter Herbert Edward Jacques m. 5 September 1936 **Edna May Bell**
b. 17 October 1910   b. 26 March 1915
d. 31 May 1942
Children
Walter Herbert Jacques married 26 October 1968 **Pamela Joy Ward**
b. 4 October 1937   b.
Children
Paul Gregory Jacques   married 10 February 1995 **Tracy Anderson**
b.19 November 1972
Children
Amanda Marie Jacques
b. 22 April 1994
Antony Shane Jacques
b.3 March 1979

Loraine Ethel Jacques   married 31 October 1959   **Anthony Bartlett**
b.1 September 1941
Children
Michael John Bartlett   married 10 October 1981 **Debbie Nardin**
Kerry Lorraine Bartlett married 12 November 1983 **Tony Van Moorsel**
Children
Ashlee Lorraine Van Moorsel
b. 26 November 1985
Leah Halene Van Morsel
b.14 March 1988

Thomas Edward Jacques
b. 23 March 1913
d 4 April 1924

<u>Gordon Stanley Jacques</u> married 19 December 1936   **Ethel Ellen Murphy**
b. 14 December 1914   b. 11 February 1917
d. 4 April 1995   d. 4 July 1987
Children
<u>Ronald Jacques</u>   married   **Thelma**
b.11 July 1938
Children
Martin Jacques
b, 1982
Renae Jacques
b. 1985

<u>Valerie Ethel Jacques</u>   married 19 December 1959 **Robert Adair**
b. 10 July 1940   b. 3 March 1939
Children
Sharon Yvette Adair   married 6 May 1978   **Louis Carro**
b. 6 August 1960
Children
Shantelle Carro
b. 1 December 1981
Janelle Carro
b.12 January 1984
Troy Carro
b.19 December 1985
Rachelle Carro
b.2 May 1988

Russell Adair
b. 29 July 1963
d. 29 July 1963
Fiona Joy Adair   married 1983   **Wayne Mitchel Nelli**
b.10 November 1965
2nd marriage 1991 **Arthur Trosti**

Sue-anne Margaret Adair married 15 November 1986   **Sym Darroch**
b. 2 February 1968
Children
Joshua Gordon Darroch
b. 14 December 1988
Jessica Mary Darroch
b. 31 December 1992

Jodie Maree Adair
b. 29 May 1974

<u>Gloria Wendy Jacques</u> married 27 October 1962 **John Anton Sanders**
b. 4 September 1943   b. 1943
                                       d. 27 March 1970

Children
Bradley John Sanders married **Ann**
b.13 May 1963

Children
Benjamin Sanders
Nicholas Sanders

Susan Sanders   married 22 December 1991 **Peter Williams**
b. 20 August 1966

Gloria Wendy Jacques   2nd. marriage 1972   **Lester Paige**
children
Melissa Paige
b. 15 June 1979

<u>**Alfred George Jacques**</u>   married 6 November 1948 **Olga Laudy**
b. 18 September 1918
d. 6 February 1987
Children
<u>Jennifer Jacques</u>
b. 1956
Children
Aaron Jacques
b. 22 July 1988

<u>Peter Jacques</u>
b. 1958
Children
Blanco Jacques
b.3 January 1988
Justin Jacques
b.24 February 1990
David Jacques
b. 2 September 1992

<u>**Albert George Jacques**</u> 2nd. marriage 7 January 1978 **Dothory Martin**
b.17 September 1912
d. 10 August 1997

The line of Julia Ann Boxhall

Julia Ann Boxhall   married 9 February 1898 **Richard Patrick Maher**
b.21 december 1878   b. 1866
d.13 May 1967   d. 28 October 1928

Children
Mary Margaret Maher
b. 28 March 1899
d.15 September 1924

Norah May Maher   married 6 April 1929 **Kenneth James Christopher**
                                                                Kenney
b. 1 December 1901   b.28 May 1905
d. 6 June 1987
Children
Kenneth Martin Kenney   married 26 December1953 **Beryl Joyce McLauchlan**
b.11 July 1930   b.20 February 1936
d.15 August 1994
Children
Charmaine Joyce Kenney   married 1985   **Albert Radzevicius**
b. 14 September 1955   b. 15 July 1941
Children
Amy Coleen Radzevicius
b. 10 September 1986
Adam Scott Radzevicius
b. 18 November 1991

Stephen Harold Kenney
b.9 September 1957

Ronald James Kenney   married 3 October 1987 **Doris Vandalam**
b. 21 February 1960

Noeline Beryl Kenney   married 1986   **Bradley Chinnery**
b. 1 December 1962

Sheila May Kenney   married 25 September 1954 Gavin Francis Drew
b. 21 November 1931   b. 12 March 1931
Children
Melinda Catherine Drew   married 1983   **Bradley Ashcroft**
b. 1 December 1964
Children
Bradley Gavin Ashcroft
b. 16 August1983
Hayley Marie Ashcroft
b.9 February 1985

Melinda Catherine Drew   2nd marriage 1992   **David Maslen**
b.28 December 1963

Children
David Lionel Maslen
b. 28 May1991
Samantha June Maslen
b. 6 January 1993
Jayden Nicholas Lee Maslen
b. 16 November 1994
Jesse Jacob Maslen
b.6 December1996

Corinne Patricia Drew
b. 17 July1966

<u>William James Kenney</u>   married 13 June 1959   **Beryl Dunn**
b. 15 May 1938
Children
Brenda Kenney   married 6 May 1989   **Richard John Lavander**
b. 29 May 1961   16 December 1965
Children
Emma Kate Lavander
b. 16 July 1985
Danial John Lavander
b.9 November 1988
d. 10 November 1988
Zoe Sharee Lavander
b. 21 November 1989
Cassy Maree Lavander
b. 1 May 1991
Shane Michael Lavander
b. 16 November 1992
Samantha Jane Lavander
b. 14 October 1993
Shenee louise Lavander
b. 11 October 1994

Bevan Andrew Kenney   married 6 June 1992   **Susan Kathleen Robinson**
b. 9 November 1962   21 April 1963
Children
Benjamen Alexander Kenney
b. 31 March 1994
Joshua Andrew Kenney
b. 25 November 1995

Sean Peter Kenney   married 30 March 1991   **Susan Frances Page**
b. 2 February 1965
Children
Jordan Michelle Kenney
b. 25 July 1993
Nathan John Kenney
b. 20 January 1995

<u>Thelma Norah Kenney</u> married 15 July 1961 **Lesley John Walker**
b. 21 April 1941 b. 30 August 1936
Children
Noel JohnWalker and Heather Larsen
12 November 1961 d.
Children
Nicolle Ann Walker
b. 17 December1989

Leanna Jane Walker married 6 April 1985 **Mario PaolaImola**
b. 31 March 1963 b.11 November 1964
Children
Michael John Imola
b. 28 October 1988
Paul Daniel Imola
b. 5 November 1991

Dale Patrick Walker
b. 15 November 1968

<u>Patricia Ann Kenney</u> married 25 November 1961 **Bryan Adamson**
b. 12 April 1943 23 September 1941
Children
Debra Ann Adamson married 28 February 1983 **Stephen James Heath**
b. 19 May 1962 b. 13 January 1963
Children
Damien James Heath
b. 10 September 1984
Matthew Dean Heath
b. 2 January 1988
Ashley Michael Heath
b. 20 July 1991

Donna Marie Adamson married 6 August 1982 **Bryan McIntyre**
b.10 June 1963 7 August 1959
  Children
Eammon IanMcIntyre
b. 6 January 1983
Calan David McIntyre
b. 26 October 1984
Cameron Rhys Mc Intyre
b.25 May 1988
Keith Travis McIntyre
b. 8 february 1990
Brittany Marie McIntyre
b.15 January 1995
Sioban Eryn McIntyre
b. 19 May 1997

Paul Bradley Adamson married 29 March 1986 **Melanie Jane McLure**
b.10 March 1965 b. 20 October 1962
Children
Reece Brian Adamson
b.21 January 1989
Claire Elise Adamson
b.8 June 1991

Michelle Jane Adamson married 12 August 1989 **Lee Anthony Hutton**
b. 8 February1968 6 April 1967
Children
Jaymen Lee Hutton
b. 5 December 1989
Justin Michael Hutton
b. 17 June 1993

Christina Rose Maher married. 1934 **John Hamilton Greenhill**
b. 1 August 1904 d. 1972
d. 27 June 1991
Children
John Hamilton Greenhill married12December1956 **Evelyn Frances Margetts**
b.October 1934
Children
Christine Faye Greenhill married May 1979 **Ron Delvecchio**
b. 19 September 1959
children
John Michael Delvicchio
b. 6 January 1980
Ronda ChristineDelvicchio
b. 11 March 191981
David Anthony Delvicchio
b. 27 November 1987
2nd. marriage 1987 **Alan Reginald Dovey**

Anne Elizabeth Greenhill married 16September1988 **Steven John Thomson**
b. 19 September 1962
Children
Jacob Charles Thomson
10 April 1989

Thomas Hamilton Thomson
b. 7 december 1990

Evelyn June Greenhill married 1992 **Peter Mead**
b.19 September 1965
Children
Luke Mead
b.1992

Judith Ann Greenhill married 1960 **Colin Neil McQeen**
b. October 1936

Children
Shaun McQueen
b. 1962
d. 1962
Campbell McQueen   married 1988   **Helen O'Neil**
b.1966
Children
Shane McQueen
b. 1993
Tamara McQueen
b. 1996

<u>James Thomas Maher</u>   married   **Olga Amy Stockbridge**
b. 25 March 1907   b. 24 July 1898
d.9 September 1989   d. 26 November 1976

<u>Gertrude Veronica Maher</u>   married 1938   **Victor Ernest Cteretko**
b. 2 November 1909
d. 22 June 1980
<u>Gertrude Veronica Maher</u>   2nd Marriage 1951   **Kevin John ONeil**
Children
<u>John Victor Ctercteko</u> changed name
<u>John Victor Brennan</u>
b. 20 March 1940
<u>Glennys Blanche Ctercteko</u>   married 24 August 1963   **Ian Lockwood Barry**
b.20 May 1941   b. 6 January 1941
Children
John Lockwood Barry   married 3 June 1987   **Lynette Vickey Parie**
b. 28 June 1965   b. 11 November 1967
Children
Jade Ashley Barry
b.29 December 1989
Skye Tiffeny Barry
b.19 December 1990
John Lockwood Barry and **Kristina Bartley**
Children
Tristan John Barry
b. 23 July 1996
Skyanne Barry
b.13 February 1998

Loryn Leanne Barry   married 5 June 1987   **Peter Glen Rosser**
b.1 May 1967   b. 29 december 1960
Children
Peter Glen Ian Rosser
b.2 August 1988
Aricia Leigh Woolhouse Rosser
12 October 1990

Glen Ian Barry   married 21 February 1991   **Lisa Marie Hagen**
b. 5 November 1968   b.13 January 1971

Children
Kaitlyn Marie Barry
b. 2 June 1989
Mathew Lockwood Barry
b. 22 December 1995

Richard Patrick Maher married 21 February 1959 **Mary Marjorie Jacobs**
b. 10 March 1912   b. 3 June 1930
d. 13 July 1990   d.16 January 1979
Children
Richard James Maher
b. 24 April 1960
David John Maher
b. 29 January 1962
Loraine Ann Maher   married   **Timothy Ernest Skinner**
b. 13 November 1963   **b. 28 March 1956**
Children
Jessica Ann Skinner
b. 29 December 1983
Alisha Maree Skinner
b.20 July 1985
Annette Louise Skinner
b.9 December 1988
Jasmine Anita Skinner
b. 3 October 1992

Karen Marie Maher   married   **Alan James Maynard**
b.15 August 1967   b. 18 march 1962
Children
James David Maynard
b. 25 November 1994
Erin Jayne Maynard
b. 17 January 1997

Kathleen Rose Maher   married 1 July 1939   **Augustine Joseph Clune**
b. 6 May 1915   b. 1 June 1902

Children
Brian Joseph Clune
b.6 February 1940

Veronica Mary Clune married 30 November1964 **Graeme KennethWhitehorn**
b.27 April 1941
Children
Michelle Ann Whitehorn married 30 April 1988   **Kevin Redfern**
b. 26 May 1965
Children
Brendon Redfern
b. 26 August 1990
Kelsey Redfern
b.11 November 1994

Helen Louise Whitehorn
b. 9 October 1966

Nicole Maree Whitehorn
b. 5 October 1969

<u>James Thomas Clune</u>
b. 24 March 1945

<u>Yvonne Catherine Clune</u>   married 2 December 1967   **Brian John Hodge**
b. 18 May 1945   d. 5 August 1986
Children
Erica Josephine Hodge
b.20 September 1970
Michael Robert Hodge
b. 23 September 1974

<u>Susan Treasa Clune</u>   married23 November 1974   **Kenneth George Thompson**
b. 27 April 1955
Children
Antony Ian Thompson
b. 23 February 1976
Neil Joseph Thompson
b. 1 November 1979

<u>Raymond Thomas Maher</u>
b.31 August 1917
d. 13 June 1995

<u>Teresa Veronica Maher</u>   married 16 January 1947   **Lawrence Bisile**
b.4 May 1920
Children
Kathleen Bernadette Basile married 23 November 1968 **Colin John Dunn**
b.14 February 1948   b.14 June 1948
                                                d. 20 July 1978

Children
Narelle Jayne Dunn and **Michael Ian Mclaren**
b.6 April 1971
Children
Alec Ian John McClaren
b. 28 May 1999

Stephen Paul Dunn
b. 25 October 1972

<u>Teresa Veronica Maher</u> 2nd marriage 4 September 1953 **Denis Russell**
b. 4 May 1920   b. 13 April 1925
Children   d 24 February 2000
<u>Marilyn Joy Russell</u>
b. 27 October 1953
<u>Peter John Russell</u>   married 1 February 1975   **Maree Blanche Casserly**
b.3 October 1955   b.7 October 1955

Children
Karen Anne Russell   married 11 January 1997 **John Johnson**
Children
Damion Robert Johnson
b.8 July 1998

Rodney Peter Russell
b.29 March 1979
Dennis John Russell
b.16 July 1983

Maryanne Russell   married 4 December 1976 **Stephen Acton**
b.21 June 1957   b.27 May 1953
Children
Shaun Stephen Acton
11 July 1986
Brett Acton
b. 3 December 1987

Julia Ethel Maher   married 3 October 1944 **Angus Gordon Edwards**
b.7 September 1924   b.13 February 1914
                                                          d. 5 December 1997

Children
Richard Stanley Edwards   married 23 July 1971 **June Margaret McCarthy**
b. 9 February 1945
Children
Graeme Paul Edwards
b.4 January 1972
Christine Michelle Edwards
b.2 January 1975
Mark Richard Edwards
b. 12 June 1976
Amanda Jane Edwards
b.5 April 1978
Gordon John Edwards
b.15 September 1981

Allan Thomas Edwards   married 22 June 1972 **Andrea Lynne Jackson**
b. 5 June 1946
Children
Thomas Craig Edwards
b. 11 April 1976
Katrina Annette Edwards
10 January 1979

Alfred John Edwards   married 11 October 1974 **Lorraine Barbara Brophy**
b. 30 April 1948
Children
Derek Paul Edwards
b. 4 December 1979
Peta Kylie Edwards
b. 8 May 1982

<u>Gordon Douglas Edwards</u>   married 10 November 1974 **Susan Margarey**
                                                          Colley

b. 14 May 1954
Children
Tania Michelle Edwards
b. 1 April 1975
Amanda Jane Edwards
b. 5 April 1978
Gordon John Edwards
b. 15 September 1981

<u>Alban Michael Edwards</u>   married 17 July 1982 **Dianne Sharron**
  Raxworthy
b. 29 November 1951
Children
Danial Mathew Edwards
b.10 October 1982
Rebecca Lee Edwards
b. 2 June 1985
Melissa Jane Edwards
b. 15 January 1987

<u>Jennifer Lee Edwards</u>   married 17 July 1982 **Peter John Shumack**
b.29 November 1961
Children
Michael John Shumack
b. 9 February 1986
Geoffrey Paul Shumack
b. 20 July 1988

The line of Elizabeth Mary Boxhal

Elizabeth Mary Boxhal married 10 March 1909 **William Butler**
b.26 November 1881   b10 July 1876
d.   d.
Children

Margaret Mary Butler
b. 21 July 1909
d.1916

Mary Ann Butler
b. 22 March 1911
d, 10 May 1912

John Patrick Benedict Butler
b. 28 September 1912
    d. 2 August 1920

Joseph Thomas Butler
b.21 July 1914

Scolastica Butler
b. 21 July 1914

Patrick Benedict Butler
b. 16 January 1919

Augustine Butler
b. 29 December 1921

Thomas Joseph Butler
b. 25 February 1923

Bibliography

Aveling, Marian Ed., *Westralian Voices Documents in Western Australian Social History* University of Western Australia Press, Nedlands, 1979.

Bain, OP. Mary Albertus, *Ancient Landmarks.* University of Western Australia Press, Nedlands, 1975.

Bateson, Charles, *The Convict Ships 1787-1868* A.H. and A.W. Reed. 1974.

Bean, C.E. W., *The Official History of Australia in the War of 1914-1918, The A.I.F. in Franae:1917.* University of Queensland Press, 1933.

Bourke, D. F., *The History of the Catholic Church in Western Australia 1829-1979*, Vanguard Service Print, Perth, 1979.

Bourke, Michael J., *On the Swan. A History of the Swan District of Western Australia.* University of Western Australia Press, Nedlands, 1987.

Bryant, Sir Arthur, *English Saga,* Collins, Fontana Books, London, 1961.

Crowley, F.K. and B. K. de Garis, *A Short History of Western Australia,* MacMillan of Australia, South Melbourne, 1971.

_____*Australia's Western Third* MacMillan and Co. Ltd., London, 1960.

Cannon, Michael, *Who's Master? Who's Man?,* Penguin Books Australia Ltd., South Yarra, 1971.

Collette, Colonel H.B., *The 28th. A Record of War Service,* The Public Library, Museum and Art Gallery of Western Australia, Perth, 1922.

Dickens, Charles, *Great Expectations,* facsimile reproduction edition, Marshal Cavendish Ltd., 1986.

_____ *American Notes and Pictures of Italy,* Oxford University Press American Branch, New York.

Emsley, Clive, *Crime and Society in England 1750-1900*, Longman Inc. New York, 1987.

Erickson, Rica, ed., *The Brand on His Coat Biographies of some Western Australian Convicts*, University of Western Australia Press, Nedlands, 1983.

_____ *The Bicentennial Dictionary of Western Australians Volumes 1-4,* University of Western Australia Press, Nedlands, 1988.

_____ *Convicts in Western Australia 1850 - 1887 Dictionary of Western Australia, Vol XI*, University of Western Australia Press, Nedlands, with Gillian O'Mara, 1994.

_____*The Victoria Plains,* Lamb Paterson Pty. Ltd., Osborne Park, 1971.

Evans, A.G., *Fanatic Heart A Life of John Boyle O'Reilly,* University of Western Australia Press, Nedlands, 1997.

Herington, John, *Air Power over Europe 1944-1945,* Canberra Australian War Memorial, 1963.

Hasluck, Dame Alexandra, *Unwilling Emigrants: A Study of the Convict Period in Western Australia,* Angus and Robertson Ltd., 1969.

Hassam, Andrew, *Sailing to Australia Shipboard diaries by nineteenth-century British emigrants,* Melbourne University Press, Melbourne, 1995.

Hawkins, David T., *Bound for Australia,* Library of Australian History, North Sydney 1988.

Maughan, Barton, *Australia in the War 1939-1945, Tobruk and El Alamein,* Canberra Australian War Memorial, 1966.

Mayhew, Henry and John Binny, *The Criminal Prisons of London.* Frank Cass and Co., London 1968, first published 1862 .

Moore, George Fletcher, *Diary of Ten Years of an Early Settler in Western Australia,* University of Western Australia Press, Nedlands, 1978.

Morris, Norval and David J. Rothman eds., *The Oxford History of the Prison - The Practice of Punishment in Western Society .* Oxford University Press Inc., New York, 1998.

Longmore, Captain, C., *Eggs-A-Cook,* The Colortype Press Ltd., Perth 1921.

_____ *Carry On,* Western Mail, Imperial Print, Perth, 1921.

O'Brien, John, *Around the Boree Log,* Angus and Robertson, Sydney, 1950.

O'Brien, Patrick and Webb, Martyn, eds. *The Executive State,* Constitutional Press Pty. Ltd., Perth, 1991.

O'Mara, *Gillian, Convict Records of Western Australia* Friends of Battye Library Inc. Perth, 1990.

_____ *Convicts in Western Australia 1850 - 1887 Dictionary of Western Australia, Vol XI* with Rica Erickson, 1994.

O'Reilly, John Boyle, *Moondyne Joe. A story from the Underworld,* P. J. Kenedy & Sons, New York, 1879.

Denis, Richard and J. W. Hunt, *An Illustrated History of Modern Britian 1783-1964,* Longmans Green and Co. Ltd., London, 1965.

Russo, George, *Lord Abbot of the Wilderness,* The Polding Press Melbourne, 1980.

Shaw, A. G. L., *Convicts and the Colonies .* Faber and Faber, London, 1966.

Stannage, C. T. ed., *A New History of Western Australia,* University of Western Australia Press, Nedlands, 1981.

Stone, Derrick I. and Donald, S. Garden, *Squatters and Settlers,* A.H.& A.W. Reed Pty. Ltd., Sydney, 1978.

Stormon, S.J. E.J. ed. and trans. *The Salvado Memoirs,* University of Western Australia Press, Nedlands, 1978.

Thomas, M. W. ed., *A Survey of English Economic History,* Blackie & Son, Glascow, 1966.

INDEX